*Library Manager's Guide to Hiring
and Serving Disabled Persons*

Library Manager's Guide to Hiring and Serving Disabled Persons

Kieth C. Wright

and

Judith F. Davie

McFarland & Company, Inc., Publishers
Jefferson, North Carolina, and London

British Library Cataloguing-in-Publication data are available

Library of Congress Cataloguing-in-Publication Data

Wright, Kieth C., 1933–
   The library manager's guide to hiring and serving disabled persons
/ by Kieth C. Wright and Judith F. Davie.
      p.   cm.
   [Includes index.]
   Includes bibliographical references.
   ISBN 0-89950-516-3 (lib. bdg. : 50# alk. paper) ∞
   1. Libraries and the handicapped.   2. Handicapped—Books and
reading.   3. Handicapped—Services for.   4. Handicapped—Employment.
I. Davie, Judith F., 1942–   .   II. Title.
Z711.92.H3W75   1990
025.5′277663—dc20   89-43637
                                                                              CIP

Manufactured in the United States of America

McFarland & Company, Inc., Publishers
  Box 611, Jefferson, North Carolina 28640

Table of Contents

v

Introduction

The authors of this book have previously written about library and information services for disabled persons and have presented numerous workshops concerning library services for the disabled. This volume is distinguished from the previous works in focusing on the library as a total system, not exclusively on library public services for the disabled.

This idea arose from a concern that most published works discussing library services for disabled persons deal only with the public-service aspects of the library: having materials in appropriate formats, communicating with the disabled in ways that are understandable, and creating access to the physical facility of the library. While library public services are important to disabled persons, creating a library where the services are integrated with other programs and services involves the library as a total system. This book focuses on all of the critical aspects of the library system that can affect the services offered to disabled persons and their ability to use the library. Each chapter looks at a critical component in the library system's service to disabled persons, raises questions and responds to them, and provides practical suggestions and resources for further consideration of each area. References are found at the end of each chapter. The appendixes give names, addresses, and telephone numbers of national organizations for disabled persons, publishers, and vendors. Where organizations are cited in the text, only the name of the organization is listed. Full information will be found in the appendixes.

A brief summary of each chapter follows.

1. **Staff Development.** Because staff attitudes determine the level and quality of services available to disabled persons, the first chapter considers the roles of the library director and professional staff in modeling appropriate attitudes and planning and implementing staff development. Specific suggestions are made for staff-development

resources and activities, and the involvement of disabled persons in the process.

2. **Recruiting, Selecting, and Hiring Disabled Persons.** The heart of better library services for disabled persons lies in affirmative-action employment. Only as the library becomes a place where the disabled and others have daily routine contact as coworkers will library services for disabled persons (and nondisabled persons) improve. Affirmative action is defined; the concept of task and workplace analysis is introduced (with forms); and appropriate technological devices are presented.

3. **Selection and Acquisition of Materials.** Materials and formats appropriate to disabled persons' interests are not always easy to find. This chapter is divided into two parts: (a) selection criteria and sources for materials portraying disabled persons for use in the general collection of the library; (b) appropriate formats for materials for disabled persons and sources of materials for acquisition. The chapter also points out the utility of various materials-conversion activities.

4. **Organizing the Library Collection for Accessibility.** Providing information for disabled persons in an integrated fashion is discussed. Subject cataloging is subject to cultural lag in acceptable terminology because the language changes faster than librarians can adopt new subject-heading terminology, check out cross-references, and modify catalog cards. The chapter next discusses awareness of stereotypes in subject description, the need for up-to-date subject headings, and the need to revise cross-reference structures to allow easy access to needed information. Finally, the chapter discusses the need for an accessible structure for the catalog and the uses of technology in that effort.

5. **Making the Library Facility Accessible.** The authors believe that as staff and supervisory attitudes change in relation to disabled persons, there will be improved access to materials and services for disabled persons. However, some special modifications in physical facilities and services will be needed. This chapter describes some of the basic facility modifications that may be needed: parking, building access, service and work-area access, lighting, furniture arrangement, sign systems, and personal areas.

6. **Public Service Programs.** This chapter describes the integration of disabled persons into library programs and services. A strong case is made for *integrated* rather than specialized services for disabled persons. Included is a discussion of various delivery systems for those who cannot get to the library building. The reference process with disabled persons is next discussed, including potential communication barriers, specialized reference sources relevant to information needs of disabled persons, and the potentials and problems of information and referral services and referral files.

Library systems develop a variety of special collections of materials often related to local or family histories. Most of these collections pose particular problems for disabled persons because of the fragile condition of the materials, storage facilities, and lack of available materials in a usable format. Possibilities for providing information services in such collections for disabled persons are described. A final section of this chapter discusses public-service programs involving access to materials available in other collections, which are now provided through on-line bibliographic services and regional networks. As library systems plan for such services, the need for access for disabled persons needs to be part of that planning.

   7. **Information Services.** The rapid pace of technological and information change and its effect on disabled persons are the focus of this chapter. Electronic publishing, full text retrieval, and various adaptive devices for microcomputers are described.

   The appendixes list relevant organizations, vendors, and research facilities, and provide a subject, person, and agency index to the book.

   A final note about language: Obviously, the controversy over defining *disability* or *handicap* will not be settled by this book. Some writers argue that *disability* means the medical condition and that *handicap* refers to the status of the individual as a result of disability. Other writers define *disability* as an inability to do things that affects the whole person and define *handicap* as a specific, clearly limited condition. Readers who are interested in the controversy over terminology and its impact on disabled persons will find extensive discussion in Burgdorf (1980). Legal definitions abound, some courts taking the position that the *Webster's Third* definition of *handicap* is to be used: "a disadvantage that makes achievement unusually difficult." The Rehabilitation Act Amendments of 1974 produced a definition of *handicapped person:*

> any person who (i) has a physical or mental impairment which substantially limits one or more major life activities, (ii) has a record of such an impairment, or (iii) is regarded as having such an impairment. U.S. Code, SS706(7)(B)(Supp. V 1981)

   The authors have chosen to use the term *disabled person(s)* in preference to *handicapped, crippled,* or the newer term *physically challenged.* In this decision we follow the practice of major advocacy groups of disabled persons and the United Nations.

REFERENCES

Burgdorf, R. L., Jr., ed. 1980. *The legal rights of handicapped persons.* Baltimore: Brookes.

1

Staff Development: Involving the Whole Library Staff in Developing Services to Disabled Persons

The role of the library director and staff supervisors is crucial in determining whether a library system serves disabled persons. If the librarians under the leadership of the director are sensitive to the needs of disabled persons, the entire library staff will assume that such sensitivity is the "normal" thing. If the librarians are either ignorant or insensitive, the rest of the staff will adopt those attitudes in dealing with staff recruitment, materials selection, facility design and arrangements, library programs, and patrons.

INITIATING CHANGE IN STAFF ATTITUDES

The library director must initiate staff-attitude change. Since many of the attitudes related to disabled persons are at the unconscious level, library directors and their professional staff will have to engage in "consciousness raising" concerning their individual (and group-reinforced) attitudes. Just as many male supervisors have been surprised to discover their real attitudes toward women in professional staff positions, so librarians will be surprised and made uncomfortable by their attitudes toward and opinions about disabled persons.

Prior to any attempt to modify staff attitudes, the director and the professional staff should examine their own attitudes toward disabled persons. One way to assure such examination is to "preview" staff-development activities and materials as a professional staff prior to utilizing these activities and materials with the rest of the staff. A large number of staff-development activities and audiovisual materials are available. An annotated list of some of these activities and materials will be found at the end of this chapter.

1

TAKING THE INITIAL STEPS IN CONSCIOUSNESS RAISING

The realization that all people have stereotypes concerning other people is an essential first step in any attitude change. Disabled persons face stereotypes because many individuals grow up without daily face-to-face contact with disabled peers. Disabled persons then become "strangers" who are unknown, and individuals create stereotypes to deal with these strangers.

Prejudice and discrimination are complex social interactions that distort social relationships by overemphasizing some characteristic of a group (such as race, gender, sex, age, or disability) and finding socially acceptable ways to justify this overemphasis. Feagin and Eckberg (1981, p. 2) provide an analytical diagram of prejudice and discrimination having the following dimensions: (a) motivation, (b) discriminatory action, (c) effects, (d) the relationship between motivation and action, (e) the relationship between action and effects, (f) the immediate organizational context, (g) the larger social context. Since prejudice has so many dimensions, it is unlikely that there is any quick or simple solution. This book is designed to assist library managers and staff in overcoming the multidimensional problems of discrimination and denial of access to persons with disabilities.

Library directors and professional staff members may not be able to deal with all of these complex factors, but they can deal effectively with the immediate organizational context of the library by demonstrating attitudes that are not discriminatory and by developing library staffs, collections, and programs that recognize disabled persons.

Involving disabled persons in the planning and delivery of any staff-development activities related to disabled persons is one way to assure reexamination of attitudes. If a member of an organization or advocacy group of persons with disabilities is involved in planning discussions and decisions, the professional staff is forced to deal with that individual as a peer who has expertise to offer and not as a disabled person. Many communities and school systems already have advisory panels or committees made up of disabled persons and their advocates. Members of these groups are often willing to work with the library in staff-development activities. State and local committees on the employment of the handicapped often have members who are willing to serve in such advisory roles. Contact the President's Committee on the Employment of Persons with Disabilities for a listing.

Local school systems often have staff-development activities related to the "mainstreaming" of disabled children into regular classrooms. The staff-development coordinator of the local school system or the staff-development director of the state education agency will often be good sources of information about materials, activities, and disabled persons who are willing to serve in advisory roles.

Basic research on attitudes toward disabled persons has been conducted by Yuker, Bock, and Younng (1977). They found that an individual's attitudes toward physically disabled persons were similar to the
individual's attitudes toward the aged, the mentally ill, or different racial
groups. Yuker (1986) reviewed twenty-five years of research utilizing the
Attitudes Towards Disabled Persons Scales (ATDP), including the reli-
ability and validity of the scales and the social desirability of the various
attitudes of respondents. English (1977), Schroedel (1979), and Stubbins
(1977) present overviews and summaries of attitude-toward-disability
studies.

Because staff-attitude change begins at the top, the steps to overcoming stereotypes listed below begin with self-examination by the library
director and the professional staff of the library. Once the director and the
staff have examined their own stereotypes, planning can begin for staff-
development activities that may change the stereotypes of the rest of the
staff and governing boards of the library.

FACING THE DIFFICULTIES IN CHANGING ATTITUDES

Individuals without knowledge of or contact with disabled persons develop
unrealistic expectations and attitudes about those persons. In 1960, Wright
coined the term *spread* to describe the most harmful general attitude
developed about disabled persons. Spread happens when an individual
meeting a disabled person assumes that the person not only has a disability
but is disabled in all areas. The reader can observe this happening when
people raise their voices in conversation with a blind person, when the
waiter asks what a blind friend will have without speaking to the blind person, or when someone makes funny facial contractions speaking to a deaf
individual. Spread tends to depersonalize the disabled person into "one of
those" (Velleman, 1979, p. 5). Roth (1983) notes that the "stigma" attached
to disabilities is often focused on a negative factor—the inability to do
something, the absence of something. More positive attitudes focus on
what the individual *can* do. Moving from "loss" to "capabilities" is a crucial
part of staff-development activities.

Another difficulty facing supervisory staff is the experience of library
staff of "normal" library services. Almost all staff members will have
practical or educational experience with library systems in action. Unfortunately, most of that experience will have been in libraries designed,
organized, and operated as if there were no disabled persons in the society.
In the same way, transportation, buildings, furniture, and various types of
equipment have been designed, created, and advertised as if disabled persons were not around. Staff members usually do not have the experience of

accessible facilities, accessible formats of information, or a genuine concern for seeking, acquiring, and making information available in a nonoffensive manner. It is very difficult to teach people about something they have never experienced.

PROVIDING INFORMATION AND CONTACT TO CHANGE STAFF ATTITUDES

Changing staff attitudes can be done successfully in two ways: (1) increased knowledge of disabling conditions and their effects on individuals, (2) increasing contact with disabled persons. A combination of contact and knowledge will probably be most effective. The research on attitude change has been summarized by the authors (Wright and Davie, 1983) as well as Dequin, (1983, chap. 4). In 1988, Yuker edited an excellent summary of research about attitudes toward persons with disabilities entitled *Attitudes toward Persons with Disabilities*. The staff-development activities that follow have been used by library associations, library education programs, and individual libraries to promote a more realistic attitude toward disabled persons.

OVERCOMING STAFF STEREOTYPES A STEP AT A TIME

Self Assessment

Everyone has stereotypes about other people. It is important that the library supervisory staff examine their own attitudes about disabled persons. There is a tendency for well-educated individuals to have a good knowledge of the "right" vocabulary to use in discussing various disabling conditions; however, their emotional attitudes toward specific disabilities may be colored by previous experience, disabilities within family history, or total lack of contact with a particular disability. Uneasiness around disabled persons may also reflect deeper psychological fears; disabilities may be seen as evidence of everyone's vulnerability to death, disease, and injury. People may be forced to face unpleasant truths about themselves or their environment (Safilios-Rothschild, 1977).

Attitude Change through Information

Since some stereotypes arise out of what has been called the ignorance of isolation, the presentation of up-to-date knowledge about disabling conditions, the abilities of disabled persons, and the need for access to facilities and information in appropriate formats can reduce some stereotypes. Since disabled persons have been historically isolated from the rest of society, ignorance about disabling conditions and the abilities of disabled persons abounds. Bowe (1978, p. x) says:

> Disabled people have been out of the mainstream of American life for two hundred years. And these years have seen the construction of modern American society — its values, its heritage, its cities, its transportation and communication networks. So that now, when they are coming back into our society, the barriers they face are enormous.

Individuals who are ignorant of disabilities are not usually intentionally prejudiced. There are sources of accurate, up-to-date information on disabling conditions and the real-life situations of disabled persons. Some of these include the following (addresses in Appendix A):

- **American Deafness and Rehabilitation Association.** Ask for their catalog.
- **Disability Rights Center, Inc.** Ask for their "How well do you understand disability?" a true-false test (75 cents).
- **The National Rehabilitation Information Center.** A special library of information on disability and rehabilitation with its own on-line database.
- **National Easter Seal Society.** Ask for their "Portraying Persons with Disabilities in Print" as well as their publications list.
- **National Information Center on Deafness, Gallaudet University.** Ask for their catalog of materials.
- **National Library Service for the Blind and Physically Handicapped.** Ask for "Building a Library Collection on Blindness and Physical Handicaps; Basic Materials and Resources" as well as a list of other reference bulletins.
- **National Organization on Disability.** Ask for copies of REPORT and a listing of their materials on Community Partnership Programs as well as other publications.
- **The National Technical Institute for the Deaf.** Ask for their "Catalog of Valuable Products and Resources."
- **The President's Committee on the Employment of Persons with Disabilities.** Ask for the list of governors' committees and the latest quarterly report.
- **Regional Rehabilitation Research Institute on Attitudinal, Legal, and Leisure Barriers.** Ask for their "Barrier Awareness" series.
- **Rehabilitation International, USA.** Ask for their film catalog.

Other national organizations listed in Appendix A will also have accurate, inexpensive information materials.

Attitude Change through Simulation

Some stereotypes arise from fear of anything different or any person seen as not a member of one's group. These "different-therefore-dangerous" stereotypes are often found in reactions to persons of other races, age groups, or sexual orientation. Kriegel's "Uncle Tom and Tiny Tim" (1969) points out the similarities and differences in the stereotyping of minority-group members and disabled persons. Some disabling conditions cause individuals who have these conditions to appear to be different. The physically disabled, the individual with cerebral palsy, Down's syndrome, muscular dystrophy, the blind or visually impaired, can usually be identified visually as "not like me." Deafness and hearing impairment have been called invisible disabilities because these disabling conditions are not immediately obvious to the casual observer.

A part of the problem of "strangeness" arises from our society's history of institutionalizing persons judged to be different. Early patterns of family, religious-order, or community care of disabled persons gave way in the nineteenth century to institutional care in large custodial facilities *away* from the local community (President's Committee, 1976). Wolfensberger (1969, p. 143) points out:

> Whether young or old; whether borderline or profoundly retarded; whether physically handicapped or physically sound; whether deaf or blind; whether rural or urban; whether from the local town or from 500 miles away; whether well behaved or ill behaved; we took them all, by the thousands, 5000 to 6000 in some institutions. We had all the answers in one place, using the same facilities, the same personnel, the same attitudes, and largely the same treatment.

Stereotypes arising from psychological fears of difference are not readily reduced through sharing information about disabilities; these attitudes must be modified through experience of disabling conditions and contact with disabled persons. A partial answer may be found in simulating disabling conditions in staff workshops. Preschool teachers are often told that viewing the classroom from the perspective of the student can be helpful, so they sit on the floor to get a child's-eye view of the various work and play areas. In a similar manner, staff members can simulate various disabilities. Wright (1988) stresses that the simulation experience should assist the participants in finding out not only what *cannot be done* but also what *can be done* by the person with a specific disability.

Some ideas for simulation exercises:

Visual Impairment and Blindness. Simulations of visual impairments can be created by using glasses with paper tubes glued on (tunnel vision) or a lens fully or partially taped over with translucent tape. A microfilm reader adjusted to be just out of focus is a good simulation of some visual difficulties. Remember that blindness is not typically like having on a blindfold; few legally blind persons are totally without light response. Such simulations can be supplemented with films such as

- *What do you do when you see a blind person?* 1971. American Foundation for the Blind.
- *Not without sight.* 1973. American Foundation for the Blind.
- *What color is the wind?* Alan Grant Productions.
- *The blind participate.* 1981. Lawren Productions.

Simulation experiences and film viewing should focus on the wide variety of visual impairments and their effects on both the visually impaired person and the sighted person who encounters a visually impaired individual for the first time.

Hearing Loss and Deafness. Simulations of the effects of hearing loss are available as recordings (see list below) or can be simulated with special earplugs in combination with noise-reduction headphones. Wearing such earplugs, staff members should try to buy something in a store, talk on the telephone, or listen to a large group discussion. Covering the ears *does not* simulate deafness. Many people are surprised to find that deaf or hearing-impaired persons do not live in a silent world. Several records and films are available that simulate the auditory effects of hearing loss:

- *Getting through: A guide to better understanding of the hard of hearing.* 1971. Chicago: Zenith Corporation.
- *How they hear: The sounds of abnormal hearing.* 1964. Northbrook, IL: Stowe Associates (record, pamphlet, 10 slides).
- *The deaf communicate.* 1981. Mendocino, CA: Lawren Productions (16mm, 12 min.).

Hagemeyer (1979) discusses the myths associated with the words *deaf, mute, deaf and dumb,* and the wide variety of educational experiences that deaf and hearing-impaired persons may have had.

Physical Handicaps. Have staff members utilize a wheelchair or wear a full-length fiberglass leg or arm cast and try various regular activities such as entering a building, using a table, getting information at the circulation desk. Such experiences of frustration can help staff members appreciate how libraries are designed as if disabled persons did not exist. Several films may be useful follow-ups to simulation exercises:

- *A day in the life of Bonnie Consolo.* 1976. Pasadena, CA: Arthur Barr (16mm, color, 16 min.). See also the new film *Bonnie Consolo:*

*A woman born without arms tells her inspiring story of deter-
mination and poise.* 1986. Barr Films (16mm, or video, 23 3/4
min.).

- *I'll find a way.* 1978. Toronto: National Film Board of Canada (16
mm, color, 30 min.).
- *Walk a while in my shoes.* 1974. Toronto: National Film Board
of Canada (16 mm, color).

A Final Note.   As Hallenbeck (1984) and Selvin (1979, p. 117) note,
a warning about all simulations is needed. Simulations are essentially
"games" that people play for a short time. Even the group experiences of
"trust" often used in nonverbal-communication workshops of "outward-
bound" types of training are *only* simulations. Games that allow an individual to experience some of the frustration caused by a disabling condition to one of the senses *do not* give the true experience of most disabilities
because when the game is over, the individual voluntarily ceases to be
disabled. Disabled persons *live* with their disabling condition and learn to
function in spite of that condition. Most of these people cannot voluntarily
stop being disabled.

CONCLUSION: TAKING THE NEXT STEPS

A typical way of dealing with the fear of difference has been to assume that
difference means *inferiority.* Those "others" are necessarily deserving of being ignored, pitied, or despised because they are inferior. So long as disabled people remain an unknown group without individual characteristics,
they can be stereotyped as inferior. If disabled people are encountered in
situations where the staff member is in a superior position, the usual
stereotypes can be maintained—and may even be reinforced because the
staff member can maintain a pseudopaternalistic attitude of helpfulness
based on pity. Even well-meaning people like and love others in the wrong
way when they see themselves as "above" or "more fortunate" than the objects of their feelings.

   This superior-inferior situation can be changed by appointing a disabled person to the advisory or governing board of the library. The ongoing
contact with the library system will provide that individual with many opportunities to raise questions about programs, policies, and procedures
that affect disabled persons. The contact with that individual as a "supervisor" will be beneficial to the director of the library and the professional
staff.

   The most effective attitude-changing activity that the library director
and librarians can promote is the recruitment and selection of disabled

persons as members of the professional staff of the library. When staff members encounter disabled persons as board members, consultants, legal advisors, or county commissioners, they are forced to deal with a real person in a professional role who incidentally has a disabling condition. For this reason, Chapter 2 deals with the recruitment, selection, and hiring of disabled persons for library positions.

STAFF-DEVELOPMENT MATERIALS

Against all odds. 1981. Lauran Productions, Ltd.; 16mm, 25 min., color.
> Three physically disabled people discuss their accomplishments and barriers they have overcome.

Bookbinder, S. 1978. *Mainstreaming: what every child needs to know about disabilities.* Boston: Exceptional Parent Press.
> Describes the activities of the Meeting Street School to foster acceptance of children with disabilities.

Bower, E. M., ed. 1980. *The handicapped in literature: A psychosocial perspective.* Denver, CO: Love.
> Presents excerpts from fiction and nonfiction works that depict people with different disabilities. Each excerpt is accompanied by commentary and questions for discussion.

Brightman, A. J. 1984. *Ordinary moments: The disabling experience.* Baltimore: University Park Press.
> Disabled persons write about their everyday life experience in a society full of intentional and unintentional barriers.

Cheaver, R. C., and Cheaver, G. C. 1975. *Laugh with Accent.* Bloomington, IL: Accent Special Publications.
> Cartoons of the problems disabled persons face in attitudes and accessibility. Excellent discussion starters.

Dewar, R. L. 1982. Peer acceptance of handicapped students. *Teaching Exceptional Children* 14, 188–193.
> Describes a St. Charles, Missouri, program to enhance the acceptance of disabled children by their peers. Suggests inexpensive materials to use in similar programs.

Dobo, P. J. 1982. Using literature to change attitudes toward the handicapped. *Reading Teacher* 36(3), 290–292.
> Describes ways teachers can use children's literature to overcome children's fears of disabilities and accept their disabled peers. Use of children's-literature techniques with adults is nonthreatening and often very useful.

Elliott, T. 1983. Celluloid images of disability. *American Rehabilitation* 9 (October, November, December): 12–15.
> Discusses the media image of disabilities, summarizes other media studies, and offers guidelines for constructive portrayals of disabled persons.

Emerging. n.d. Ottawa: Canadian Rehabilitation Council for the Disabled; 16mm, 40 min., color.
> The evolution of public awareness in attitudes toward disabled persons and progress in rehabilitation technology and architectural design.

Gartner, A., and Joe, T. 1986. *Images of the disabled, disabling images.* New York: Praeger.

Examines the presentation of disabled persons in various media formats, the impact of public policy of these images, and addresses strategies for developing appropriate policies. A good discussion starter.

Hague, P. 1984. *Responding to disability: A question of attitude.* St. Paul: Minnesota State Council for the Handicapped, 208 Metro Square Building, St. Paul, MN 55101.

A question-and-answer format to stimulate thinking about attitudes toward disabled persons; divided into two sections: (1) fourteen questions related to situations and possible responses, (2) discussion of responses.

Jernigan, K. 1984. Blindness; the circle of sophistry. *The Braille Monitor* (August): 353–364.

Describes myths and stereotypes about blind persons and how these are maintained.

Kamien, J. 1979. *What if you couldn't . . . ? A book about special needs.* New York: Scribner's.

Written to answer children's questions about persons with disabilities. Useful with adults who often have similar questions and are shy about asking them.

Kilburn, J. 1984. Changing attitudes. *Teaching Exceptional Children* 16 (Winter): 124–127.

A program, "Better Understanding of Handicapped Children," is described, including activities for different age groups, including adults.

Konczal, D., and Pesetski, L. 1983. *We all come in different packages.* Santa Barbara, CA: The Learning Works, P.O. Box 6187, Santa Monica, CA 93160.

Although designed for children three to six years of age, these activity suggestions, slightly restructured, will work well with library staff and board members.

Lovejoy, E. 1982. Attitudes — the worst barriers. *Information Reports and Bibliographies* 11:3, 5–8.

Program suggestions for library programs to overcome negative attitudes of librarians and trustees.

Makas, E. 1981. *Attitude and disability.* Washington, D.C.: Regional Rehabilitation Research Institute on Attitudinal, Legal and Leisure Barriers.

A literature review on attitudes toward disabled persons, including a section of attitudes of employers and co-workers.

Maloff, C., and Wood, S. W. 1988. *Business and social etiquette with disabled people: A guide to getting along with persons who have impairments of mobility, vision, hearing or speech.* New York: Charles Thomas.

One Giant Step. n.d. Ottawa: Canadian Rehabilitation Council for the Disabled; 16mm, 40 min., color.

Shows the range of available technical aids and how they are used by disabled persons.

Randall, M. 1983. This "mill" expands comfort zones. *Disabled USA* no. 4, 1–3.

Description of a training program, "Windmills," that provides workshops on attitude change toward disabled workers.

Sensitivity to the disabled patron. n.d. Baltimore: Library Video Network, 1811 Woodlawn Drive, Baltimore, MD 21207. Videotape, 29 min.; $50 for seven-day rental, $115 purchase.

Disabled persons talk frankly about the barriers they face in libraries and how these barriers can be broken down.

White House Conference on Handicapped Individuals. 1977. *Volume One:*

Awareness Papers. Washington, D.C.: Author.
Essays by experts on the social aspects of disability, with emphasis on attitudes.

REFERENCES

Bowe, F. 1978. *Handicapping America.* New York: Harper and Row.
Dequin, H. C. 1983. *Librarians serving disabled children and young people.* Littleton, CO: Libraries Unlimited.
English, R. W. 1977. Correlates of stigma towards physically disabled persons. In Stubbins, J., ed., *Social and psychological aspects of disability.* Baltimore: University Park Press, 218–219.
Feagin, J. R., and Eckberg, D. L. 1981. Discrimination: motivation, action, effects, and context. *Annual Review of Sociology* 6, 1–20.
Hagemeyer, A. 1979. Special needs of the deaf patron. In Velleman, R., *Serving physically disabled people: An information book for all libraries.* New York: Bowker, chap. 7.
Hallenbeck, C. E. 1984. The trouble with simulation. *The Braille Monitor* (October 1984): 486–487.
Kriegel, L. 1969. Uncle Tom and Tiny Tim: Reflections on the cripple as negro. *American Scholar* 38 (Summer) 412–430.
President's Committee on the Employment of the Handicapped 1976. Disabled Americans: A history. *Performance* 27 (5, 6, 7) (November–December 1976) (January 1977).
Roth, W. 1983. Handicap as a social construct. *Society* 20 (3), 56–61.
Safilios-Rothschild, C. 1977. Prejudice against the disabled and some means to combat it. In Stubbins, J., ed., *Social and psychological aspects of disability.* Baltimore: University Park Press, 265.
Schroedel, J. 1979. *Attitudes toward persons with disabilities: A compendium of related literature.* Albertson, N.Y.: Human Resources Center.
Selvin, H. C. 1979. The librarian and the blind person. In Velleman, R., ed., *Serving physically disabled people: An information book for all libraries.* New York: Bowker, 116–139.
Stubbins, J., ed., 1977. *Social and Psychological Aspects of Disability.* Baltimore: University Park Press.
Velleman, R. A. 1979. *Serving physically disabled people: An information book for all libraries.* New York: Bowker, 1979.
Wolfensberger, W. 1969. The origins of our institutional models. In Kugel, R. B., and Wolfensberger, W., eds., *Changing patterns in residential services for the mentally retarded.* Washington, DC: The President's Committee on Mental Retardation.
Wright, B. 1977. *Disabling myths about disability.* Chicago: National Easter Seals Society.
_____. 1988. Attitudes and fundamental negative bias: Conditions and corrections. In Yuker, H. E., *Attitudes toward persons with disabilities.* New York: Springer, 3–21.
Wright, K. C., and Davie, J. F. 1983. *Library and information services for handicapped individuals.* 2d ed. Littleton, CO: Libraries Unlimited.
Yuker, H. E. 1986. *Research with the Attitudes Towards Disabled Persons Scales*

(ATDP) 1960–1985. Hempstead, NY: Hofstra University Bookstore, Hempstead, NY 11550. (ERIC Document Reproduction Service, ED 278 195).

_____, ed. 1988. *Attitudes toward persons with disabilities.* New York: Springer, 3–21.

Yuker, H. E., Bock, J. R., and Younng, J. H. 1977. *The measurement of attitudes toward disabled persons.* Albertson, NY: Human Resources Center.

2

Recruiting, Selecting, and Hiring
Disabled Persons
for Library Staff Positions

The most effective means of changing attitudes and effecting change in library services so that disabled persons may be served is through affirmative action. Affirmative action requires a careful analysis of the tasks performed in the library, an understanding of essential workplace modifications, and a willingness to seek out qualified persons to fill positions.

This chapter will explore the meaning of affirmative action in the library context, the values of affirmative action for library staff and patrons, the legal requirements for affirmative action, the impact on the work environment of the library, starting a library affirmative-action program, essential job modifications for disabled workers, sources of assistance in developing an affirmative-action program, adaptive devices and technology for disabled workers, recruiting disabled applicants, and giving hiring preference to disabled applicants.

THE MEANING OF AFFIRMATIVE ACTION FOR
LIBRARY MANAGERS

Because peer or superior relationships with persons who are disabled are so critical to successful staff-attitude changes, the authors are strong advocates of affirmative action in all levels of employment in the library and in all appointments to boards or advisory groups serving the library and the community. Without presenting a series of legal definitions or tracing the long struggle waged by disabled persons and their advocates for equal rights under the law, *affirmative action* may be defined as action taken to promote opportunities in employment and professional associations for those who have been traditionally denied full employment and full participation in the life of our society. For disabled persons, this denial has taken the form of inaccessible facility and workplace design, social stigma, and various legal strategies of exclusion from education, training, and career counseling. Affirmative action is *not* equal opportunity, but rather a conscious attempt by the library director and the professional staff to

- understand and overcome negative attitudes about hiring and promoting disabled persons;
- define jobs and design work areas with necessary access and equipment levels, so that qualified disabled persons can apply for and do the job;
- recruit qualified disabled persons for these positions through traditional and nontraditional sources;
- give preference in hiring to disabled persons when qualifications of those persons and other candidates are equal;
- train present staff so that they can work effectively with employees who have disabilities.

THE VALUES OF AFFIRMATIVE ACTION

Obviously the authors of this book think that affirmative action pays significant dividends for the library staff and for the services the library provides. American Library Association policy is also committed to affirmative action:

> The American Library Association is committed to equality of opportunity for all library employees or applicants for employment, regardless of race, color, creed, sex, age, physical or mental handicap, individual lifestyle, or national origin; and believes that hiring disabled individuals in all types of libraries is consistent with good personnel and management practices. (*ALA Handbook of Organization,* 1986, p. 235)

Beyond policy, one major reason for recruiting disabled persons is that there are so many of them. Neff (1985) cites statistics that show the following numbers of such persons:

Hearing impairments:	17 million
Orthopedic impairments:	18 million
Visual impairments:	8.2 million
Speech impairments:	2.1 million
Missing extremities:	1.6 million
Completely or partially paralyzed:	1.2 million

More recently, the President's Committee on the Employment of Persons with Disabilities (1985) published a similar study of disabled adults in

America. If libraries ignore 48.1 million persons, they ignore a very large number of possibly qualified individuals for positions in libraries.

The other major benefits of affirmative action relate to improving staff performance and library services. If staff members have prejudiced attitudes toward *any* group, that prejudice is likely to influence the type of service offered to anyone who is identified as "different" or "strange." Daily routine contact with a wide variety of persons makes for healthy attitudes toward the self and toward other persons, including "strange" or "new" library patrons.

THE LEGAL REQUIREMENTS FOR AFFIRMATIVE ACTION

Cottam (1987) has recently summarized what he calls the "dizzying array of acts" related to equal employment opportunity and affirmative action. He includes a brief analysis of court cases and administrative interpretations related to affirmative action in relation to race, sex, age, handicapping conditions, and Vietnam-era veterans. Basically, the law related to employment of disabled persons is found in Section 503 of the Rehabilitation Act of 1973 and the subsequent regulations issued to enforce that legislation. Disabled persons may take legal action if

- they have reason to suspect that they have been denied employment on the basis of disability;
- when that disability does not affect performance of the announced job responsibilities or
- where reasonable accommodation would make performing the job possible.

Furthermore, employing institutions are enjoined from recruiting, selection processes, job definitions, or placements that can be shown to discriminate on the basis of disability.

Central to the legal rights of disabled persons is the Rehabilitation Act of 1973 (P.L. 93-112, 87 Stat. 355) and its amendments in 1978 (P.L. 95-602, Tit. I, 92 Stat. 2955, see various sections of 29 U.S. Code). The act and its amendments were intended to increase employment skills and the ability of disabled persons to lead independent lives *and* to prevent discrimination from frustrating these efforts.

Title V of the Act (29 U.S. Code, Sections 791-794c, 1976, and Supp. V., 1981) establishes a national civil-rights policy for disabled persons. Section 504 of Title V states:

No otherwise qualified handicapped individual in the United States . . . shall, solely by reason of his handicap, be excluded from participation in, be denied the benefits of, or be subjected to discrimination under any program or activity receiving Federal financial assistance or under any program or activity conducted by any Executive agency or by the United States Postal Service.

Discrimination is broadly interpreted to include

- practices that directly or indirectly deny opportunities;
- afford opportunities that are unequal;
- require different or separate opportunities;
- use criteria for selection or methods of administration that have the effect of discriminating.

All recipients of federal funding must provide assurances of compliance with Section 504 and must conduct a self-evaluation of their compliance in practice. Programs are to be run so that they are readily accessible to and usable by handicapped persons.

Section 503 of the act requires businesses with federal contracts of $2,500 or more to take affirmative action to employ and advance qualified handicapped individuals. Federal contracts must contain clauses prohibiting employment discrimination against qualified handicapped persons. The regulations define a qualified handicapped person as one who "is capable of performing a particular job, with reasonable accommodation to his handicap." Again, federal contractors are required to do a self-analysis of their efforts in affirmative action with relation to handicapped persons.

A detailed analysis of the statistics of discrimination against disabled persons, federal laws, and the regulatory definitions related to these issues is found in the U.S. Commission on Civil Rights publication *Accommodating the Spectrum of Individual Abilities* (1983) and in Mathimatica Policy Research, Inc., *Digest of Data on Persons with Disabilities* (1984). Readers interested in the legal aspects and definitions are also referred to the article "Affirmative Action for Librarians and Library Workers Who Are Handicapped" (Wright, 1983) or "Section 504 and the New Civil Rights Mandates" (*Amicus,* 1977). The specifics of the "500 series" federal regulations will be found in the *Federal Register* for Wednesday, May 4, 1977, Part IV. The National Council on the Handicapped (1986) has assessed current federal laws and programs affecting disabled people and made legislative recommendations for improvement in definitions and responsibilities in numerous areas.

THE IMPACT OF AFFIRMATIVE ACTION ON WORK

Although often unasked, the question of how hiring disabled individuals will affect overall work performance is certainly on the minds of many supervisors and their coworkers. People without regular experiences with disabled persons often assume that disabled persons will have to be "carried" by other employees, and supervisors worry about the effect of the disabled person on job productivity. The Harris organization did a major survey of top managers concerning employing disabled persons in 1986. They found that the vast majority of managers and employers rated disabled persons as "good" or "excellent" workers and that there were very few costs associated with hiring disabled persons.

STARTING AN AFFIRMATIVE-ACTION PROGRAM

The library director, the governing board, and the professional staff will need to agree that the library-staffing patterns are to reflect the totality of society and that disabled persons have a right to participation in that society. If there is agreement among staff and governing boards, the library should adopt a formal policy statement concerning affirmative action. This starting point is very easy to write about but very difficult to accomplish. Yet without this first step, very little will be accomplished, and what is accomplished may be destroyed by what is said or done at a later date. The library director must take the time to educate governing boards and the library staff in understanding disabilities and seeking to overcome past employment practices.

When the library director and governing board are committed to an affirmative-action program with regard to recruiting and hiring disabled persons, they will need to face the fact that many library supervisors will still have difficulties in the process of recruiting, interviewing, and selecting qualified applicants who happen to be disabled in some way. Employer attitudes *do* affect employment. The President's Committee on Employment of Persons with Disabilities has repeatedly found that disabled persons want to work and that an estimated 60 percent of the more than 11 million disabled persons would never succeed in finding permanent employment (PCEPD, 1975, 1986). Many disabled persons are forced to stay in dead end jobs far below their ability levels. There are a number of negative attitudes which can affect the process of affirmative action. The Office of Personnel Management (1979, pp. 9–10) has listed the following examples:

> Apathy—Many people are unaware of the problems that confront handicapped employees and applicants. Therefore, they do not care about these problems and do not work to solve them.
> Paternalism—People with the best intentions may nonetheless have the mistaken idea that handicapped individuals cannot take care of themselves, that they need special supervision on the job, and that a great deal of time must be spent meeting their needs.

Focus on Disability—When a handicapped individual is considered for a job or promotion, it is easy to overemphasize what the individual will be unable to do.

Fear—Many people are uncomfortable around individuals with certain disabilities. They are afraid because the other person is different, and they are embarrassed by their response to this difference.

Curiosity—Some interviewers who have no intention of offering jobs interview handicapped persons out of curiosity. This practice is unfair and insulting.

Stereotyping—Preconceived notions interfere with consideration of individual characteristics. That some deaf people are good printers does not mean that other deaf people should be forced into that occupation.

Fear of Change—Employers may be afraid that bringing a handicapped person into an office or a shop will disrupt normal routine and lessen efficiency or productivity. This is especially true if the job that is open has not previously been held by a handicapped person.

Focus on Superstars—Disabled persons are sometimes placed in positions for which they are overqualified, and therefore they perform in an above average manner. Employers may then come to expect "superstar" performance from every disabled worker rather than the normal range of performance.

Misinformation—So-called "facts" should be scrutinized carefully, as many widespread beliefs are erroneous. Employment opportunities often are spoiled by misinformation.

Backlash—Some managers and supervisors resent what they feel is pressure to employ and promote handicapped individuals and members of other special populations.

Since these problems exist in many employment situations, library directors and professional staff should guard against the tendencies to insist,

- "*We* do not discriminate against anyone on the basis of handicap, but our jobs require normal functioning in all areas." (The handicapped as librarians. 1968. *Wilson Library Bulletin.*)
- "Handicapped persons will impose burdens on the rest of the staff." Even if the staff has not been consulted!
- "Job restructuring is very difficult if not impossible, and we have always done it this way."
- "Let such persons work in facilities and programs for the handicapped. Isn't there a Goodwill Industries here?"

When a library staff decides to undertake an affirmative-action program in relation to persons with disabilities, initial efforts should be directed toward job definition, recruitment, and hiring of disabled persons for professional positions, so that the impact of affirmative action is not diluted. Hiring a disabled person as clerk or custodian or page does not have the same impact as hiring a professional staff member to catalog, direct a branch, or provide reference services.

JOB MODIFICATIONS TO ACCOMMODATE DISABLED WORKERS

Given the current state of libraries' use of computer technology, job-description and schedule modifications have become commonplace in libraries. The same principle applies to affirmative action: Now that the library has decided to hire qualified disabled persons for staff positions, what modifications are needed in job requirements, worksites, and schedules?

In some cases, the arrangement of work areas may be required, so that disabled persons can get to the work area and function there. It is often easier (and less expensive) to move a job to a more accessible location than it is to create access at the present jobsite. Chapter 5 discusses the various basic facility-design decisions which the library director and staff will need to make if disabled persons are to work in the library or become library users. In this chapter, the focus will be on recruitment of qualified applicants who are disabled, the interview and selection process, and the job modifications necessary to accommodate the applicant and the staff member once hired.

Since library directors and supervisors have had limited experience with job accommodations, the following examples of simple accommodations of tasks in the workplace may be helpful.

Carrying and Lifting of Objects

There are no jobs that are totally free of lifting/carrying tasks. Persons with balance problems, stamina limitations (from stroke or heart conditions), motor impairments (from spinal cord injuries, cerebral palsy, amputations) may have difficulties with lifting and carrying. Lower-back problems are the most common difficulty encountered in lifting and carrying; redesign of the tasks involved in a job can prevent many of these problems.

Objects to be lifted and carried are too heavy or bulky:

- assign tasks to more than one person;
- break up load into several containers;
- use lifts, carts, or dollies;
- modify task from lifting to lowering, from lowering to carrying, from carrying to pulling, from pulling to pushing (depending on disability);
- assure firm grip with handles, hooks, etc.;
- minimize container weight (change from wood to plastic, wood to paper, etc.);

- avoid load shifting inside container (pack full);
- change container shape, so that container can be carried close to body;
- use large wheels or casters on carts;
- minimize friction, so that objects can be slid and not lifted and carried.

Many tasks require moving materials and audiovisual equipment on some type of cart. These carts should be carefully evaluated since some of them have a tendency to tip over if pushed from the wrong point on the cart. Other book carts assume that people can work within 12 inches of the floor. The weight of materials (books, files, equipment) will often require careful evaluation. No one tries to move a ten-year accumulation of the CBI, but people do try to move reference materials that are very heavy. Technology in the form of CD/ROM and on-line access may transform some of the object lifting and moving, but many libraries will have essential information in heavy, cumbersome packages for some time to come.

Objects Are Inaccessible to Workers:

- locate work objects 20–52 inches above floor where possible;
- locate objects on the same level as that to/from which they must be moved;
- when object assembly is required, make all sides of assembly accessible by using turntables or chairs on wheels;
- avoid situations where one-handed lifting is possible;
- provide height-adjustment worktables, storage, and seating;
- eliminate deep storage containers by use of spring-loaded or gravity-feed containers.

Work areas need to be larger and more accessible in most situations. The ability to turn a "lazy Susan" so that necessary tools, books, and equipment are at hand is not just a convenience for disabled library workers. Often such work stations allow two or more people to share reference materials, a microcomputer terminal, microfiche readers, and so forth.

Frequency or duration of lifting/carrying causes fatigue:

- allow more time;
- reduce frequency of task;
- rotate personnel on task;
- allow rest periods;
- screen workers to fit job.

(These guidelines were compiled from Ayoub, 1982).

Often, tasks can be simplified in easy ways, such as collecting tools and equipment in one place, eliminating unnecessary motions, changing the sequence of tasks to increase efficiency, using simple mechanical devices, and examining the work environment to see that proper physical support is provided. In libraries, much lifting and carrying are involved in moving materials to and from their storage areas (usually shelves in stacks). Some library tasks in inaccessible stacks with very high or very low shelves will require that materials be brought to the disabled worker and returned to the shelves by another person. In open-stack situations, where disabled patrons and workers are supposed to have access to materials on the shelves, thought will have to be given to stack-area redesign and layout (see Chapter 5).

Getting from One Place to Another (Mobility)

Persons with disabilities sometimes have difficulty walking long distances, climbing stairs, avoiding obstacles. Mobility issues are related not only to the specific worksite but also to the parking lot, building entrances, elevators, bathrooms, and other facilities for personal hygiene. Basic accommodations include

- Parking lot:

  - reserve parking spaces close to workplace for disabled persons;
  - provide signs designating special parking;
  - enforce parking regulations;
  - make spaces 12 feet wide.

- Building entrances:

  - build ramps (ANSI standards 1 foot rise in 12 feet);
  - use portable ramps where possible;
  - install a wheelchair lift (maximum lift usually 8 feet);
  - widen entrance doors to 36 inches;
  - change door hardware from knobs to levers;
  - consider automatic or powered door openers.

- Workstations:

  - provide desks, tables that are adjustable;
  - move storage and shelving to "within reach";
  - provide storage for walking aids (crutches, walkers, canes, wheelchairs);
  - make safety plans known to all (how does the disabled person get out without the elevator?);
  - modify climate controls for remote operation.

- Floor conditions:

  - use special waxes of a nonskid variety;
  - install traffic-route nonskid materials;
  - use special wheelchairs, three-wheel motorized scooters;
  - replace high-pile, tacked-down carpet with firm-pile, glued-down, rubber-backed carpet.

Seating for Workers

Almost every library job requires seating. Often, the seating requirements include moving from one seated location to another. In some circumstances the work areas (circulation desk, catalog, vertical file) require seating that is higher (or lower) than "normal" seating. Proper seating reduces fatigue and back and hip problems, and conserves energy. A good chair can add as much as forty minutes of production to a workday.

In general, seating should be on a fully adjustable chair, so that height, distance, angle, and rotation of the seat can be controlled by the individual. If these controls are powered, many disabled persons will be able to utilize the seats. In some disability situations, the worker may need to work in a supported standing position for a portion of the day. This requirement will mean that workstations of desks must be useful at an erect standing position (or adjustable to that position). Since many temporary disabilities (accidents, surgery, pregnancy) will require seating and workstation adjustments, the library supervisors should think about making all seating and workstations adjustable. Eastman Kodak Company (n.d.) has published a guide to designing workplace seating, and Roschko (1982) includes seating and table designs for the disabled and elderly in his book *Housing Interiors for the Disabled and Elderly.*

SOURCES OF ASSISTANCE ON JOB-DESCRIPTION MODIFICATION, WORKSITE ANALYSIS

A basic source of assistance is the disabled person(s) in the community. If the library advisory committee or board has disabled persons as members, these individuals can assist the library in reviewing job descriptions and worksites for potential barriers to employment of disabled persons. Often, local government agencies have an office that is in charge of job and worksite analysis, and can assist with this task. In larger cities there will be a mayor's committee on the employment of persons with disabilities, and every state and territory has a governor's committee on the employment of persons with disabilities. These committees have members who are skilled in job redefinition and worksite modification for disabled persons.

Job analysis for disabled persons focuses on the essential physical, intellectual, and sensory skills needed for performing a particular set of job-related tasks. The Physical Demands Checklist found at the end of this chapter can be used to determine the actual skills needed for a job. The checklist includes a column for listing possible job accommodations, so that the job can be done by a disabled applicant. Often, the checklist is used in employment interviews with disabled applicants, so that the applicant can suggest possible accommodations, worksite modifications, or essential equipment. Some examples of job modifications for a variety of jobs from bakers to switchboard operators will be found in "Job Modifications" (1984).

On the national level, the Job Accommodations Network (JAN) of the President's Committee on the Employment of Persons with Disabilities is a telephone-based computer data base of specific information on how disabled persons can do individual job tasks. A call to 1-800-JAN-PCEH allows the supervisor or employer to receive brief descriptions of accommodations made in situations similar to the job being considered from human-factors consultants. There is no charge for this service, but employers are asked to share their job-accommodation efforts with JAN.

ABLEDATA is a data base of more than 14,000 commercially available aids and devices for disabled persons, including any available evaluations or consumer-feedback information. Devices cover a wide spectrum of use in work and personal life. Custom searches of the data base are provided by the National Rehabilitation Information Center (see NARIC in Appendix A). Once the library supervisors, in concert with the disabled employee, have determined that a device is needed for the job, a custom search can be requested. NARIC also prepares "State Guides," which lists the key personnel, addresses, and telephone numbers for selected rehabilitation agencies in each state. The organization provides guides, for specific disabilities, of available resources that will be useful to families and individuals wishing to know more about specific disabling conditions. Accent on Information is a private organization that offers information on 5,000 products, organizations, and resources on adapting or producing equipment.

In 1985, Mainstream, Inc. issued six publications, *Dealing with Disabled People in the Workplace.* Each pamphlet focuses on a particular disabling condition and employment considerations related to that disability. Librarians will find this series a helpful overview on interviewing, supervising, and working with the disabled. Mainstream provides a consultation service on accessibility, a national referral service for qualified disabled persons as well as seminar interviewing, and human-relations training in relation to disabled persons. Mainstream also operates project LINK (telephone), which links qualified disabled applicants with potential jobs.

There are a number of centers that specialize in rehabilitation and work or life accommodations for specific handicapping conditions. These centers include Rehabilitation Engineering Centers, Research and Training Centers, and Research and Demonstration Projects usually associated with large university programs.

ADAPTIVE DEVICES AND TECHNOLOGY

There are a wide variety of technical "devices" to assist disabled persons in performing tasks, communicating, and dealing with an inaccessible world. *Rehab Brief* (1987) recently summarized the new developments in using robots to assist disabled persons in the home and workplace. Significant developments in control (by a variety of switches) and fine motor-skill operations of robots have made a number of robotic projects possible. Disabled persons are using robots to perform daily tasks. As *Brief* points out, current financial disincentives mean that most robots are unique and therefore expensive. However, contrary to LaRocca and Turem (1978), who found a number of major barriers to the application of technology to assist disabled persons, *Brief* is optimistic about the development of afford-able industrial robotics to accommodate disabled people in the workplace. World Rehabilitation Fund (1986) gives a worldwide perspective on the development of interactive robotic aids for independent living by disabled persons. Additional assistance can be found in Baruch College (1985), Bowe (1983), and *RPG* (1982).

Prior to *any* purchase of devices, communications equipment, or ac-cessibility aids, the library staff should consult with disabled persons. Sim-ple modifications (see Chapter 5) can often be substituted for very expen-sive devices. Disabled persons may have worked out job and communica-tion accommodations that use equipment readily available in most workplaces. Because the pace of change in technological applications for disabled persons is very rapid, the following periodicals give more up-to-date information:

- *Aid and Appliance Review.* Quarterly (free). The Carroll Center for the Blind, 770 Centre Street, Newton, MA 02158.
- *Bulletin on Science and Technology for the Handicapped.* Quarterly (free). American Association for the Advancement of Science, Office of Opportunities in Science, 1776 Massachusetts Avenue, Washington, DC 20036.

- *Communications Outlook.* Quarterly ($12/year). International Action Group for Communication Enhancement. Artificial Language Laboratory, Computer Science Department, Michigan State University, East Lansing, MI 48824.
- *Rehabilitation Technology Review.* ($25/year). Rehabilitation Engineering Society of North America, 1101 Connecticut Avenue, N.W., Suite 700, Washington, DC 20036.
- *Sensus.* Sensory Aids Foundation, 399 Sherman Ave., Suite 12, Palo Alto, CA 94306 (415-329-0430).
- *SIGCAPH Newsletter.* Quarterly ($22/year). Association for Computing Machinery, Special Interest Group on Computers and the Physically Handicapped, 11 West 42nd Street, New York, NY 10036.
- *Technical Innovation Bulletin.* Quarterly ($15/year). Innovative Rehabilitation Technology, Inc., 26699 Snell Lane, Los Altos Hills, CA 94022.

Technology is rapidly changing the ways work is done and the channels used for communication. It has been estimated that 75 percent of office jobs in the future will require some use of computer-related equipment utilizing microcomputers or terminals. Butler (1984) reviews the impact of technology on electronic publication and dissemination of information. His literature review is worth consulting as library staff members think about the future ways that libraries will handle information and the impact of that handling on services to disabled persons and disabled persons as library employees.

Specific technological adaptations will depend on the particular disabling conditions; however, a wide variety of adaptive devices suitable for library jobs do exist. They include

- One-handed (left or right) typewriters and computer keyboards. Typewriting Institute for the Handicapped has Dvorak one-hand typewriters and computer keyboards (Apple II and IBM PC). They also handle a large-type typewriter for the visually impaired.
- Voice-activated computer terminals.
- Computer output devices with Braille output.
- Magnified-image screens on monitors.
- Speech-synthesis output devices that can spell or speak whatever appears on the monitor screen or in printed text. Maryland Computer Services, Inc. produces "Ready Reader," an optical character-recognition system that will scan a typed or printed page, sending signals to a computer that speaks the text a word, a sentence, or a page at a time. It has a multipage paper tray, so

that more than one page can be read at a time. Speaking speed is adjustable from 45 to 750 words a minute.

The Kurzweil machine is another example of speech-from-printed-text-fonts machines. This company also has a voice-activated typewriter as well as a series of interfaces for data entry, Braille conversion, and speech output in several languages. More recently, the company has introduced a less expensive machine with a hand-held camera that can be used to scan text.

Street Electronics manufactures a number of computer speech synthesizers, including Echo +, Cricket, and Echo PC2. These synthesizers can be programmed to provide speech output for microcomputers. The recent introduction of a second series of microcomputers by the IBM Corporation included an IBM-developed speech-recognition and speech-synthesis peripheral.

Seelman (1986) lists the following telephone-adaptive devices:

- Hearing:

  - Amplified hearing handsets that increase volume up to 30 percent
  - High-gain hearing handset that increases volume up to 45 percent

- Speech:

  - Amplified-speech handset that increases the volume of the outgoing voice up to a 20-decibel gain
  - 5C artificial larynx: a speaking aid for persons who have lost use of the larynx

- Hearing and Speech:

  - Telecommunication devices for the deaf (TDDs)

- Hearing and Vision:

  - Signalman relay: causes a plugged-in lamp to flash on and off when phone rings

- Motion:

  - Speaker phone: enables persons with mobility disabilities to use phone without handset
  - Directel: telephone user can blow in a plastic tube to place, receive, and hang up telephone calls

Sources of information on telecommunications devices and services include:

- The consumer-affairs or public-information offices of state public utilities commissions
- Regional and local telephone companies
- AT&T National Special Needs Center: 1-800-233-1222 (voice); 1-800-833-3232 (TDD)
- Tele-Consumer Hotline
- Telecommunications for the Deaf, Inc.
- Nationwide TDD Center for Long Distance Service: 1-800-222-4474 (TDD)

The increased use of CRT terminals, microcomputers, and on-line bulletin boards in libraries should increase the flexibility of many library jobs. If a disabled applicant is hired, local vocational rehabilitation centers, medical centers, and the applicant herself will be helpful in redesigning the work area and the schedule to get the job done and accommodate the disabling condition. A list of vendors of various adaptive and communication aids for computers will be found in Appendix C.

With the development of modern technological devices such as telecommunications, voice input and output for microcomputers and terminals, enhanced displays, and remote sensing devices, we can no longer say that most library jobs require full capacities in all senses or great physical strength. Many jobs can be redesigned, with appropriate equipment, to allow qualified disabled persons to perform the tasks successfully.

Disabled and nondisabled persons have the same difficulties understanding and working with CRT communications, software packages, or on-line retrieval-search strategies. Present research on robotics combined with prosthetic devices may give disabled persons advantages when it comes to physical dexterity and strength. Demonstrations of detailed, intricate microlevel work with prosthetic devices and "amplified" muscle power are found at rehabilitation research meetings.

RECRUITING DISABLED INDIVIDUALS

The process of recruitment and selection may be defeated because qualified disabled persons do not know about job vacancies or promotion opportunities. Under Section 504 of the regulations related to the Rehabilitation Act of 1973 (*Federal Register,* Wednesday, May 4, 1977), most educational institutions have made their programs accessible. Still, the total number of qualified candidates located will be small if only the traditional library recruitment sources (professional journal advertisements, state library and professional association joblines, and mailings to accredited library education programs) are used.

Alternative sources of candidates include (1) local higher-education institutional offices for services to disabled students, (2) regional, state, and local vocational rehabilitation offices and counselors, (3) centers for the training of disabled persons, such as Goodwill Industries, Industries for the Blind, (4) governor's committees on the employment of persons with disabilities. A list of such organizations will be found in Appendix A.

Job-vacancy announcements should be made available to these agencies as well as to organizations composed of disabled persons and their advocates. Much recruitment is informal and based upon personal contacts. For this reason, disabled persons on advisory committees, boards of trustees, and so forth should be informed about all job vacancies and new positions.

HIRING PREFERENCES AND THE DISABLED

Unless the library director and staff take action, it is unlikely that disabled persons will be equitably represented in any library situation — support staff or professional. The only way to overcome this inequity is to insure that a large enough pool of applicants is found and that when equally qualified persons are available, preference is given to the disabled applicant. The focus should be not only on recruiting disabled persons but also on hiring them for positions.

The greatest barrier to effective recruitment, placement, and advancement of disabled persons (and other previously excluded groups) may be found in honestly held opinions that library employers must be "fair" in their recruitment practices and show no preferences. Such opinions sound as if they have ethical bases and are very hard to overcome. In fact, the history of education, civil rights, and employment for minority groups, women, foreign-born persons, and disabled persons are replete with various kinds of "fairness" (including "separate but equal") that have ignored qualifications, equal pay for equal work, and true opportunities for personal advancement in the professions.

As a heavily female-populated, male-managed profession, the library profession should be particularly sensitive to the effects of long-term paternalistic efforts on behalf of any excluded groups. Current library employment statistics still show that the bulk of the work is done by women who are supervised by men, that men and women at the same level of responsibility or position are not paid equally, and that the opportunities for advancement for women are limited. If library directors and professional staff continue to be "fair" about the employment and promotion of women in the profession, these situations are not going to change. Disabled persons are going to be excluded from employment, underemployed, unemployed, and ignored unless someone takes up the cause of finding, promoting, and placing the disabled in career positions that will lead to promotion and positions of leadership. It is essential that the library director, professional staff, and board of trustees have a consensus on this issue if progress is to be made.

Alexander et al. (1985) have summarized good employment practices when recruiting, selecting, and employing disabled persons:

1. Involve the newly hired person in decisions on accommodations. This person is the *best* source of information.
2. Develop one staff person with special skills in placement of disabled persons. This specialist can assist in the placement and accommodation process, identify jobs that require little or no modification, and serve as a contact person for disabled employees.
3. Collect print and human-resource information on job accommodations, devices, and so forth.
4. Hold preemployment discussions or orientations with staff and supervisors. Identify who is coming, what the disabilities are, and management's job expectations. Encourage coworkers to look for ways to improve job efficiency and identify changes that are needed.
5. Share successful accommodations with other employers.
6. Seek advice and assistance from local agencies that are knowledgeable about disabled persons and their abilities.
7. Set a "tone" of commitment to accommodation of workers with disabilities.

CONCLUSION

This chapter has discussed the recruitment and selection process, various workplace accommodations that may be required, and the role of professional staff in the selection and placement process for disabled persons.

Ignoring affirmative action means the creation of a work and library environment devoid of persons who are different from us. Library professionals have a choice: They can work toward an enriched staff environment in which there is great diversity of personality and background—a greatly enriched environment—or they can continue to work and associate in a much poorer environment. Once a library staff includes disabled persons, the director and staff can focus on library operations and programs to insure that disabled persons can be included in the library. The following chapters focus on library operations (selection of materials and their organization), public programs, and facility modifications.

PHYSICAL DEMAND CHECKLIST

(Handicapped Employment Program, Ontario Ministry of Labour, 400 University Avenue, 10th Floor, Toronto, Canada M7A 1T7)

Completing the Physical Demands Checklist (see pages 32–33)

1. Complete the checklist at the jobsite, so that the physical demands of the job and the work environment can be recorded as observed.
2. Column 2: "Check if Performed": Begin the process by vertically checking those factors which are required as part of the job. Factors not required by the job should be marked with an X to indicate that they were considered and were not appropriate.
3. Each required factor will now be completed horizontally for columns 3 and 4 as follows:

   a. Column 3: "Weight Maximum (Usual)": Where appropriate, the maximum number of pounds to be moved for each factor should be recorded.
   b. Column 4: "Frequency": Record the frequency of each factor required. Range is from Never to Major (0 to4).

4. The columns marked "X" on the checklist should be verified by the work supervisor and changes noted if there are discrepancies prior to the checklist being utilized as part of job specifications.
5. Column 5: "Comments": This column indicates whether a factor can be modified. It is important to complete this column with the assistance of the work supervisor, who will be able to indicate the flexibility in the job to exchange portions of a job with a worker able to undertake a particular physical demand or to modify the job specifications. This column may also be used in the interview process to allow the disabled applicant to indicate appropriate accommodations needed to do the job.

Management Endorsement

Ensure that the completed checklist is verified and agreed to by the work supervisor.

Incorporating Physical Demands Checklist
in the Personnel System

The checklist should become part of the job specification. It can be attached to the job specification or copied on the reverse side. As job specifications are revised or new jobs developed, a physical demands checklist should be completed as part of the regular process.

Using the Information to Enhance Advertising
and Outreach Recruitment

As part of your outreach recruitment to disabled persons, include the words "Physical Demands Available on Request," or simply the access sign, in your advertisement. Many newspapers now have the access symbol, which they use in their theatre advertisements. A potential applicant can request the physical demands checklist, which is photocopied and mailed out to the applicant. In this way a disabled person can determine the appropriateness of the job requirements to his particular abilities and disabilities.

Outreach recruitment is an important factor in developing positive personnel practices related to employing disabled persons. You may find it helpful to complete the Outreach Recruitment Form (see copy) for each job for which a physical demands checklist has been completed.

The Outreach Recruitment Form utilizes information from the job specification as well as from the Physical Demands Checklist and will assist groups and organizations concerned with disabled persons in determining your needs. The Outreach Recruitment Form can be sent to local groups and organizations for a job-posting bulletin board.

Effective Interviewing, Using Knowledge
of Essential Physical Demands

The checklist becomes an interview tool and permits you to deal with specific aspects of the job as well as discussing the handicap in a specific job-related way. The checklist allows the disabled applicant to suggest compensating techniques, including worksite modifications such as lowering or raising the work level or use of technical assistance devices.

PHYSICAL DEMANDS CHECKLIST

Date   Job Title   Contact

Branch   Telephone No.   Ext.

Physical Demands	Check if Performed	Weight Maximum (usual)	Never	Seldom	Minor	Require	Major	Comments
Strength Factors:								
Lifting								
Pushing								
Pulling								
Carrying								
Fine Finger Move								
Handling								
Reaching								
Above Shoulder								
Below Shoulder								
Gripping								
Foot |1 foot								
Action |2 feet								
Mobility Factors:								
Throwing								
Sitting		X						
Standing		X						
Walking		X						
Running		X						
Climbing		X						
Stooping/Bending		X						
Crouching		X						
Kneeling		X						
Crawling		X						
Twisting		X						
Balancing		X						
Sensory/Perceptual								
Factors:								
Hearing:								
conversation		X						
other sounds		X						
Vision: far		X						
near		X						
color								
depth		X						
Perception: spatial		X						
form		X						
Feeling		X						
Reading		X						
Writing		X						
Speech		X						
Work Environment		X						
Inside Work		X						
Outside Work		X						
Hot/Cold		X						

Physical Demands	Check if Performed	Weight Maximum (usual)	Never	Seldom	Minor	Require	Major	Comments
Humid/Dry___		X						
Dust___		X						
Vapor, fumes___		X						
Moving Objects___		X						
Hazardous Machines___		X						
Electrical Hazards___		X						
Sharp Tools___		X						
Radiant/Thermal Energy___		X						
Slippery Floors___		X						
Congested Worksite___		X						
Conditions of Work Factors:								
Traveling___		X						
Working Alone___		X						
Working Independent But in a Group___		X						
Interact with Public___		X						
Operate Equip. or Machinery___		X						

Accessibility to persons using wheelchair

ESSENTIAL DUTIES (list):

NONESSENTIAL DUTIES (list):

Note: Review duties before interview.
Discuss reasonable accommodation at interview.

OUTREACH RECRUITMENT FORM

1. JOB TITLE:
2. BRANCH:
3. CONTACT: TELEPHONE:
4. HOURS OF WORK:
5. WORK ENVIRONMENT:
6. ACCESS:
7. QUALIFICATIONS:
8. JOB DUTIES:
9. PHYSICAL REQUIREMENTS:
10. OTHER WORK-RELATED DEMANDS:
11. OPPORTUNITY FOR ADVANCEMENT:
12. SPECIAL MACHINERY/EQUIPMENT:
13. FLEXIBILITY WITHIN DEPARTMENT:

REFERENCES

Alexander, D., et al. 1985. The process of designing for the handicapped worker. *Joint Seminar on Designing Jobs for Handicapped Workers.* Proceedings, Chicago, December 1985, Hot Springs, Arkansas: Arkansas Research and Training Center in Vocational Rehabilitation, Box 1358, Hot Springs, Arkansas 71902 (1302-39/1000/12-85).

American Library Association. 1986. *ALA handbook of organization.* Chicago: The American Library Association.

American National Standards Institute. 1980. *American national standard specifications for making buildings and facilities accessible to and usable by physically handicapped people* (ANSI A117.1). New York: American National Standards Institute, 1430 Broadway, New York, NY 10018.

Ayoub, M. A. 1982. *The Journal of Occupational Medicine* 24(9) (September): 668–676.

Baruch College. 1985. *Computer equipment and aids for the blind and visually impaired.* New York: Computer Center for the Visually Impaired, 17 Lexington Avenue, Box 515, NY 10010.

Bowe, F. 1983. *Reasonable accommodation handbook.* Parsippany, NJ: American Telephone and Telegraph Co.

Butler, M. 1984. Electronic publishing and its impart on libraries: A literature review. *Library resources and technical services* 28, 41–58.

Commission on Civil Rights. 1983. *Accommodating the Spectrum of Individual Abilities.* Clearinghouse Publication no. 81. Washington, DC: U.S. Commission on Civil Rights.

Cottam, K. M. 1987. Affirmative action: Attitude makes a difference. *Library Journal* 112(9), 47–50.

Eastman Kodak Company. n.d. *Ergonomic design for people at work.* Rochester, NY: Eastman Kodak.

The handicapped and librarians. 1968. *Wilson Library Bulletin,* 318–329.

Harris and Associates. 1986. *Disabled Americans' self perceptions.* Chicago: Harris and Associates, 1986. Reported in *Focus* (Spring 1987) 3. National Council on the Handicapped.

Job modifications: Case presentations of job modifications through adaptive equipment. 1984. *Aids and Appliances Review* 12 (Spring). Carroll Center for the Blind, 770 Centre Street, Newton, MA 02518.

Kamisar, H. 1979. Signs for handicapped persons. In Pollet, D., and Haskell, P.G., *Sign systems for libraries.* New York: Bowker, 212–225.

LaRocca, J., and Turem, J. S. 1978. *The application of technological development to physically disabled people.* Washington, DC: The Urban Institute.

Mainstream, Inc. 1985. *Dealing with disabled people in the workplace* (series). 1220 15th St., NW, Washington, DC 20005: Author.

Mathimatica Policy Research, Inc. 1984. *Digest of data on persons with disabilities.* Washington, DC: Congressional Research Service, Library of Congress. (Prepared under contract for the United States Office of Education, National Institute of Handicapped Research and Rehabilitation Services).

National Council on the Handicapped. 1986. *Toward independence: An assessment of federal laws and programs affecting persons with disabilities — with legislative recommendations.* Washington, DC: The Council (GPO # 052 003-01022-4; Appendix: 052-003-01023-2).

Neff, E. 1985. *Library services to physically handicapped persons: Fiscal year 1984.*

Washington, DC: Office of Educational Research and Improvement Library Programs, U.S. Department of Education (internal document).

Office of Personnel Management. 1979. *Handbook of selective placement of persons with physical and mental handicaps in federal civil service employment* (U.S. GPO no. 006-000-01093-8, OPM document 125-11-3). Washington, DC: GPO. *Note:* The Office of Personnel Management has developed specific regulations and guidelines, most of which can be found in Chapter 306, "Selective Placement Programs." Updates to these regulations will be found in the *FPM Bulletin.*

Pati, G. C., Adkins, J. I., and Morrison, G. 1981. *Managing and employing the handicapped: The untapped resource.* Lake Forest, IL: Brace-Park, Human Resources Press.

President's Committee on the Employment of the Handicapped (PCEPD). 1975. *The impact of unemployment on handicapped people.* Washington, DC: The Committee.

_____. 1976. Disabled Americans: A history. *Performance* 27 (5,6,7) (November–December 1976, January 1977).

_____. 1985. *Disabled adults in America.* Washington, DC: The Committee.

_____. 1985. *Disabled Americans at work.* Washington, DC: The Committee.

_____. 1986. *Out of the job market: A national crisis.* Washington, DC: The Committee.

Rehab Brief: Bringing research into effective focus. 1987. *Robotics and Rehabilitation* 10(2). Washington, DC: National Institute on Disability and Rehabilitation Research, Department of Education, 20202.

Roschko, B. B. 1982. *Housing interiors for the disabled and elderly.* New York: Van Nostrand Reinhold.

RPG: Rehab purchasing guide. 1982. Fort Washington, PA: IMS Communications, Inc., 426 North Washington Street, 22046.

Section 504 and the new civil rights mandates. 1977. *Amicus* 2.

Seelman, K. D. 1986. Current status of specialized telephone services and equipment for disabled people. *Hearing Rehabilitation Quarterly* 11(3), 14–16. Other Seelman papers are available from NARIC, 4407 Eighth St., NE, Washington, DC 20017.

United Nations. Division of Economic and Social Information. 1982. *Improving communications about people with disabilities.* New York: The Division (available from Rehabilitation International, 432 Park Avenue South, New York, NY 10016).

World Rehabilitation Fund, Inc. 1986. *Interactive robotic aids — one option for independent living: An international perspective.* New York: WRFIEEIR, c/o Diane Woods, 400 E. 34th St.

Wright, K. C. 1983. Affirmative action for librarians and library workers who are handicapped. In Harvey, J. F., and Dickinson, E. M., *Librarians' affirmative action handbook.* Metuchen, NJ: Scarecrow Press, 206–220.

_____, and Davie, J. F. 1983. *Library and information services for handicapped individuals.* 2d ed. Littleton, CO: Libraries Unlimited.

3

Selection and Acquisition of Materials: Audiences, Sources, and Formats

Selection of information materials involves consideration of two user groups: (1) nondisabled patrons and (2) disabled patrons, their families, and their advocates. Because the authors feel that a part of the library's role is attitude changing through programming, the first section of this chapter will deal with materials *about* disabling conditions and the disabled that are useful in programming, so that misconceptions about disabling conditions and disabled persons can be overcome. The second section of the chapter deals with sources and formats of materials useful to disabled persons, their families, and their advocates.

SOURCES OF ACCURATE INFORMATION ABOUT DISABILITIES

The library's collection must present disabling conditions and disabled persons in a realistic light. Historically, most library patrons have been isolated from contact with disabled persons, and most of the information resources in society (books, magazines, television) have omitted references to disabled persons. When these persons were included, they were often presented stereotypically. Errors of fact were often stated as medical or psychological truth. Biklen and Bogdan (1977) studied a sample of classic literature and popular current media, and concluded that there were few books and films that treated disabilities with sensitivity and accuracy. Schwartz (1977) found the same to be true of children's materials.

One of the best sources of information on disabling conditions will be the national associations for disabled persons, their advocates, and their families. A brief list of some of these associations will be found later in this chapter. A more extensive organization listing will be found in Appendix A. Numerous associations have public-information programs and produce regular lists of their own publications and recommended informational materials on disabilities. Whenever possible, librarians should try to get on the mailing list of these national associations, so that updated information can be made available to library patrons. More extensive lists will also be found in *National Organizations Concerned with Visually and Handicapped Persons* (National Library Service, 1984). Apple Computer, Inc. (1987) provides a list of organizations and companies interested in disabled children, *Resources in Special Education and Rehabilitation,* which lists organizations of (or for) disabled persons, sources of computer software and hardware, and applications of computers to specific disabling conditions.

Among the various groups producing information for the public, the following will provide valuable and accurate information concerning a number of disabling conditions:

- **Accent on Information.** Publishes *Accent on Living* (quarterly). Maintains a computerized file on assistive devices and how to help disabled persons live easier and better.
- **Alexander Graham Bell Association for the Deaf.** Promotes educational options for hearing-impaired persons, maintains an information center, and publishes *The Volta Review* and *Newsounds Newsletter.*
- **American Association on Mental Deficiency.** Publishes *American Journal on Mental Deficiency* and *Mental Retardation.*
- **American Coalition of Citizens with Disabilities.** Publishes *The Coalition* and *ACCD Action,* and disseminates information on the human and civil rights of disabled persons.
- **American Foundation for the Blind.** Publishes *Journal of Visual Impairment and Blindness.* Serves as a clearinghouse for information about blindness. Ask for their publication list.
- **American Library Association.** Association of Specialized and Cooperative Library Agencies. Publishes *Interface* and other occasional pamphlets and monographs of interest to libraries serving disabled persons.
- **American Printing House for the Blind, Inc.** Provides a listing of school textbooks in Braille, large-type, and recorded formats. Sells consumer products for blind persons.
- **Council for Exceptional Children.** Publishes *Exceptional Children* and serves as a clearinghouse for information on exceptional children. Information available on-line through various vendors as part of the Educational Resources Information Center (ERIC) network.
- **Human Resources Center.** Disseminates information and program

models, and conducts a comprehensive evaluation and training program for the handicapped.

- **National Association of the Deaf.** Publishes *The Deaf American* and disseminates a number of pamphlets and books about deafness.
- **National Easter Seal Society.** Publishes *Rehabilitation Literature* and a number of other pamphlets and studies. Supports research into the causes, prevention, and treatment of disabling conditions and advocacy efforts for the civil rights of disabled persons.
- **National Federation of the Blind.** Publishes the *Braille Monitor* and works through state and local organizations toward complete integration of blind persons into society.
- **National Information Center for Handicapped Children and Youth.** Disseminates information on handicapping conditions, special education, and related programs and services for disabled children and youth.
- **National Information Center on Deafness.** Information center with pamphlets and related materials on deafness in all of its cultural and educational aspects. Responds to direct inquiries; prepares fact sheets and articles on deafness, alerting and communicating devices and TDDs. Ask for their list, "Free and Inexpensive Materials." Also ask for Gallaudet University Press Catalog.
- **National Library Service for the Blind and Physically Handicapped.** Publishes *Talking Book Topics, Braille Book Review, News, Update.* Provides free library service of recorded reading materials for visually and physically handicapped persons. Excellent reference circulars.
- **National Rehabilitation Information Center (NARIC).** Information on all aspects of rehabilitation is collected in a special library. Provides answers to specific questions and maintains two computerized data bases: ABLEDATA (information and commercially available equipment) and REHABDATA (bibliographic information), which can be searched for a fee.
- **National Technical Institute for the Deaf.** Produces educational materials related to the technical education of hearing-impaired and deaf persons. Also supplies general educational materials related to these groups.
- **Orton Dyslexia Society.** Disseminates information and publications on the study, treatment, and prevention of dyslexia. Publishes *Annals of Dyslexia* and *Perspectives on Dyslexia.*
- **People-to-People Committee for the Handicapped.** Publishes *Directory of Organizations Interested in the Handicapped* and a newsletter.

- **President's Committee on the Employment of Persons with Disabilities.** Promotes employment opportunities for disabled persons and publishes a variety of related documents. Ask for a list.
- **Recording for the Blind, Inc.** Publishes *Recording for the Blind Newsletter* and *Catalogue of Recorded Texts* (every three years, annual supplements). Free taped educational materials with over 60,000 tapes on file for duplication.
- **Regional Resource and Information Center for Disabled Individuals.** Provides information and documents relating to physical disabilities, services and programs to disabled persons, professionals, and the public. REHABLINE is a prerecorded telephone-message system on various disability topics. A travel information center includes information on accessibility of accommodations, tourist sites, and transportation systems. Also has an ABLEDATA file on commercially available products.
- **Rehabilitation International U.S.A.** Collects, compiles, and disseminates international information on rehabilitation. Operates an International Rehabilitation Film Review Library that rents and sells rehabilitation films.

SELECTION GUIDELINES FOR MATERIALS

The following guidelines will be helpful in the process of selecting library materials that depict disabled persons:

- Selection of materials including disabled persons should be based on the same principles as selection of other materials: popular demand, literary quality, positive reviews in the professional literature. The mere inclusion of a disability or disabled person in a publication should not mark it for inclusion.
- The materials in the library should include disabled persons as a natural part of the general population. Do not select only materials in which the disability of the person is the primary focus.
- Materials that stereotype disabled persons as dependent, pitiful, or supercapable should be avoided. Tokenism should be avoided. "Now we have purchased six books about the disabled" is not a permanent solution to the inclusion of portrayals of disabled persons in the collection.
- The words used to describe or characterize disabled persons should be evaluated; for example, phrases that can demean individuals: "deaf and dumb," "confined to a wheelchair," "victim of," "poorly groomed," "slow." Although less common, watch out for "the blind beggar," "the disfigured villain," or "the insane criminal." Avoid materials that use clichés or slang

phrases such as "spastic," "egghead," "four-eyes," "gimp," "retard," "lamebrain."

• Materials should be selected that present disabled persons of all ages, races, and sex types doing regular things. Materials that overemphasize the disability, exaggerate or emotionalize the situation of disabled persons should be avoided. Disabled persons should be shown as participants in the society and not only in schools or institutions or with other persons having the same disability.

• Materials should present disabled persons interacting with others in mutually beneficial ways. The disabled persons should not be shown as always being helped by others. Communication between disabled and nondisabled persons should be natural, without embarrassment or awkwardness.

• Persons with disabilities, their parents, and their advocates should find multiple appropriate roles for persons with various disabilities in our society. Materials should have individuals and illustrations that include disabled persons as workers, community leaders, and participants in social and sports activities.

• Representation of disabled persons should be included in all levels (early childhood through adulthood) of materials in the library.

More information will be found in *Improving Communications about People with Disabilities,* 1985, New York: United Nations Division of Economic and Social Information, New York, NY 10017.

In 1977, The National Center on Educational Media and Materials for the Handicapped published *Guidelines for the Representation of Exceptional Persons in Educational Materials,* which expands on some of the selection ideas listed above. The National Easter Seal Society (2023 West Ogden Ave., Chicago, IL 60612) has a six-page brochure, "Portraying Persons with Disabilities in Print," which gives guidelines for writers who wish to include disabled persons in their writings. Librarians will find these guidelines useful in selection as well as preparation of local library public-relations materials.

SOURCES OF MATERIALS LISTS AND BIBLIOGRAPHIES

In addition to organizations, a number of good bibliographies about disabilities and disabled persons have been produced (note also the bibliographies listed under selections for children's and young adult services).

Bopp, R. E. 1980. Periodicals for the disabled: Their importance as information sources. *Serials Librarian* 5(2), 61–70.
> List of periodicals published for (and by) disabled persons.

Gibson, M. 1983. Bibliography: Library services for the blind and physically handicapped in the United States. In *That all may read: Library service for blind and physically handicapped people.* Washington, DC: National Library Service for the Blind and Physically Handicapped, 431–506.
> An updating of *Building a library collection on blindness and handicaps: Basic materials and resources.* Washington, DC: National Library Service for the Blind and Physically Handicapped, 1981, lists of basic resources (books, journals, organizations) for libraries that want to supply current information services on visual and physical handicaps.

National Rehabilitation Information Center (NARIC). 1985. *The periodical list: A guide to disability-related journals and newsletters.* 4407 8th St., Washington, DC 20017: Author.
> This publication includes information on title, publisher, frequency, and subject areas covered. In addition, NARIC offers special *Rehabilitation Research Reviews* in thirty key topic areas.

President's Committee on the Employment of the Handicapped. 1982. *Rehabilitation for independent living.* Edited by Lois O. Schwab. Washington, DC: The Committee.
> An annotated bibliography covering all aspects of rehabilitation and independent living, including overcoming a variety of barriers. Includes lists of other resources and publishers' addresses.

An update to "A reader's guide for parents of children with mental, physical or emotional disabilities." 1983. Baltimore: Maryland State Planning Council on Developmental Disabilities.
> A comprehensive reader's guide to the field, including books for children about disabled children, lists of articles, journals, organizations.

Velleman, R. A. 1980. Library service to the disabled: An annotated bibliography of journals and newsletters. *Serials Librarian* 5(2), 49–60.
> A basic listing of journals and newsletters in the fields of medical and vocational rehabilitation and special education, and journals edited by disabled persons (although dated, most of the journals on the list are still published).

SOURCES OF MATERIALS FOR CHILDREN AND YOUNG ADULTS

Disabling conditions and disabled persons should be represented in the library's children's section. There are a number of review sources for such materials:

Baskin, B. H., and Harris, K. H. 1977. *Notes from a different drummer: A guide to juvenile fiction portraying the handicapped.* New York: Bowker. 1977. See also their *More notes from a different drummer: A guide to juvenile fiction portraying the disabled.* 1984.
> A careful selection of fiction about disabled children and youth without stereotypes or excessive focus on disability.

Dreyer, S. S. 1977. *The bookfinder: A guide to children's literature about the needs and problems of youth aged 2 to 15.* Circle Pines, MN: American Guidance Service.

Covers books published to 1975.

_____. 1981. *The bookfinder: A guide to children's literature about the needs and problems of youth aged 2 to 15.* Circle Pines, MN: American Guidance Service.

Covers books published 1975-1978.

_____. 1985. *The bookfinder: A guide to children's literature about the needs and problems of youth aged 2 and up.* Circle Pines, MN: American Guidance Service.

Covers books published 1979-1982. A selection of nonfiction materials covering a wide range of life concerns of children: disability, loss, divorce. Indexed by life situation.

Friedberg, J. B., Mullins, J. B., and Sukiennik, A. W. 1985. *Accept me as I am: Best books of juvenile nonfiction on impairments and disabilities.* New York: Bowker.

A good introduction to evolution of attitudes, stereotypes, and terminology as well as critical evaluations of 350 nonfiction books for school-age children.

Glimps, B. E. 1983. Books can make mainstreaming easier. *PTA today* 8(60), 23-24.

An annotated bibliography of children's fiction selected to assist other children in understanding disabled classmates and their problems.

Lass, B., and Bromfield, M. 1981. Books about children with special needs: An annotated bibliography. *Reading Teacher* 34(5), 530-538.

A discussion of what to look for in children's books about disabled persons and an annotated bibliography of such books.

Offerman, M. C. 1984. The handicapped person: A bibliography. *Catholic Library World* 55(7), 287-289.

An annotated listing of forty books offering sensitive treatments of disabled persons.

Radencich, M. C. 1986. Literature for children and adolescents about people who happen to have a handicap. *Techniques* 2(4), 364-369.

A brief list of carefully selected stories that do not stereotype disabled children, deal exclusively with the disability, and meet the general criteria for good children's literature.

SOURCES OF MATERIALS FOR THE DISABLED ADULT

Information now comes in a bewildering array of formats. Each library staff will need to have a perspective on the adult patrons of the library. If the general service population of the library (actual or potential) contains disabled persons (which it will), the library staff needs to know as much as possible about (1) the information-use habits of the disabled and (2) the impact of particular disabilities on the ability to use the information in various formats.

Every individual has information sources. Many, isolated by disability from the traditional school-library-community-agency information sources, will not understand the ways that libraries offer information services. They may not even know what services libraries offer. Extending library public services to disabled persons will be discussed in Chapter 6, but in the selection process, it is essential to discover what sources disabled persons are *now* using to find the information they need and what types of information services are appropriate to various disabilities. In the years since World War II, rehabilitation of persons with disabilities has made great strides in assisting people to assume (or reassume) independent lives. Part of that independence arises from the ability to seek information, find it in an appropriate format for use, and get the information at a low cost. Libraries can play a role in the selection, organization, and delivery of information for disabled persons.

Information is packaged in a variety of formats, some of which are easily used by disabled persons. Librarians are no longer forced to select only print or film formats. Graphics and text materials are now available in computer-software formats on-line from remote sites, on large video disks, and in CD/ROM format. Chapter 7 discusses some of the implications of these newer technologies for library services to the disabled. Just as the change from the card catalog to some form of computer or microform display allows increased use of the catalog by disabled persons, so selection of appropriate formats will not only add variety to the library collection but also make parts of that collection accessible to disabled persons. Several formats are discussed below.

Large-Print Materials

One very useful format is large-print publications. These are not only useful to the visually impaired individual but may also be useful to others who find them easy to read without glasses or other visual aids. Sources of large print materials include

- Baker & Taylor
  652 East Main St.
  P.O. Box 6920
  Bridgewater, NJ 08807-0920

  Vendor of titles from most large-print publishers.

- G. K. Hall
  70 Lincoln Street
  Boston, MA 02111

  Think big with large print: how to promote and fund large-print services in libraries. Lythway's Large Print offers children's books through G. K. Hall.

- ISIS Large Print Books
  ABC-CLIO
  2040 Alameda Padre Serra
  Box 4397
  Santa Barbara, CA 92140-4397

  Cornerstone books is the publisher of children's books under this imprint.

- John Curley and Associates
  P.O. Box 37
  South Yarmouth, MA 02664

- LP Books, Inc.
  33 Old Main St.
  P.O. Box 299
  Bass River, MA 02664

  Overstock division of John Curley Associates (usually inexpensive).

- Thorndike Press
  P.O. Box 157
  Thorndike, Maine 04986

  Has a guild for large-print readers. Send for free catalog.

- Ulverscroft Large Print Books
  c/o Helen Boyle
  279 Bost St.
  Guilford, CT 06437

  Publishes excellent quality materials. Ask for "Good News" pamphlet.

Also look for free and inexpensive materials offered by companies, professional associations, and government agencies. Many agencies now have materials printed in larger type.

Use of printed materials is influenced by more than the size of the type (Tinker, 1963). Print display is made up of type style, type size, line leading (the white space between lines), proportional (in-line) spacing, as well as the reflective qualities of particular paper and ink combinations. Type styles are usually classed as *serif* or *nonserif,* depending on whether a fine serif line is used to finish off various letters (the letters of this text are set in a serif style). Type styles are often used to "set off" certain text from the surrounding text as in **bold** or *italic* letters. Overuse of bold or italic styles of letters tends to defeat the highlighting purpose of such text.

Type size is counted in *points,* which are 1/72 of an inch in height. A typical American newspaper is set in 8–9-point type. Figure 4.1 illustrates some of the typical type sizes (this book is in 10-point).

FIGURE 4.1   Type Sizes

This is 14-point type

This is 20-point type

This is 30-point type

Horizontal spacing between letters effects readability of text. Most typewriter and word-processor text allows the same amount of space between letters so that the *i* has the same space as the *w* or *m*. Many type-set or "daisy wheel" printers allow for proportional spacing based on the actual size of letters. Such spacing allows for greater reading speed without loss of understanding and decreases the cost of printed materials. The selection of paper stock and ink can drastically affect the ease of reading. Traditionally black ink on white paper with a minimum of reflection from the ink and a maximum of reflection from the paper have been found to allow for greater ease of reading. Reflection of light into the eyes is measured in *Munsell values* (Munsell Color, Baltimore, Maryland) or *United States Government Printing Office* values. The higher the reflective number assigned to ink or paper, the more light is reflected into the eyes. About 70 percent reflectance of paper is recommended for use with black ink. A higher reflectance (lighter stock) is required with colored inks.

When selecting print materials, the colors of inks and papers as well as the ability to read text in a variety of light intensities should be considered. Take the printed materials and try to read them with light shining from *behind* the reader, the light shining from *in front of* the reader, and in more and less light.

A few other comments on large print materials are in order. Ralph (1982) has suggested some thirty guidelines on materials for our aging population of readers, including the following:

- Serif-face type is best for general text at about 13-point size.
- Boldface and italics should be used sparingly.
- One or two points of leading (space between lines) should be used with the larger typefaces.
- Black ink on white or cream paper is most easily read.
- Paper with a dull (not glossy) finish is easier to read because it cuts glare.

- Text that changes type size too frequently is a bad choice because important information may be lost to many readers.

Library promotional and report materials can be produced in large type if some care is taken. For a donation of $10 to Better Communications (P.O. Box 1833, Silver Spring, MD), Ralph will send you a copy of his technical manual used to assist organizations in evaluating and improving their printed materials. He will also analyze three documents, newsletters, brochures, application forms, or bibliographies and make suggestions. Using pica type and enlarging it about 30 percent will produce text that is very readable. Many libraries will have access to an enlarging copy machine that can enlarge text to this degree. Others will have access to microcomputer software that will produce text of larger styles and fonts for posters and messages. Most of these textual-graphic programs will print a *very* black text on the printer. If librarians want to use enlarged copies or micro-computer-generated text, it is important to keep lines of text short (five inches or less).

Recorded Materials

Some library patrons will not be able to utilize large-print materials because of visual impairments or because they cannot physically handle the book format. For these patrons, materials are available in recorded formats.

The National Library Service (NLS) for the Blind and Physically Handicapped, of the Library of Congress, makes materials (both books and periodicals) available in Braille, flexible records, and cassettes. The equipment to utilize these materials is also available. All of the services—including the published announcements of new materials, the mailing of materials back and forth, and the equipment—are *free*. The services of NLS are available without charge to certified persons (certified by an appropriate professional) who cannot use regular-print materials. Services of NLS are available through a network of regional, state, and area library agencies. If the library staff are not sure about this service, they should contact their state library agency or NLS directly. NLS recordings are made to be played back at a very slow speed on specially designed equipment. Library patrons will need that equipment as well as the recording to utilize this service.

The National Library Service has published reference circulars on *Guide to Spoken-Word Recordings*. One of these is a general nonfiction guide. Other guides include "Educational, Professional and Self Development Materials," "Foreign Language Literature and Instruction," and "Literature." Each of these guides lists not only what is produced by the National Library Service but also other commercial and noncommercial sources of recordings. The National Library Service also publishes *Magazines in Special Media: Subscription Sources,* which lists periodicals and journals available in other than print format, the cost, and the source.

Several sources of information about spoken-word recordings and equipment are available:

Audio Cassette Newsletter
  P.O. Box 9959
  Glendale, CA 91206
    News of new cassette producers and products as well as new releases from existing producers.

Educators' guide to free audio visual and video materials. Randolph, WI: Educators Progress Service.
    Annotated list of free audiotapes, scripts, records.

Library of Congress. 1981. *Literary recordings: A checklist of the archives of recorded poetry and literature in the Library of Congress.* Compiled by J. Whittington. Washington, DC: The Manuscript Division.
    Tapes of poets reading their poems.

McKee, G., ed. 1983. *Audio cassette directory.* Guilford, CT: Jeffrey Norton.
    Annotated list of audio cassettes. Includes addresses of publishers.

Words on tape: An international guide to the spoken word. 1984. Westport, CT: Meckler.
    The *Books in Print* of tape, giving author, title, and subject access internationally.

Materials in Machine-readable Formats

As libraries have begun to use indexes and reference tools through various on-line systems (DIALOG, Bibliographic Retrieval Service, etc.), the possibilities of providing services to disabled persons have increased. Typically, on-line services and other computer-based library services have not been thought of as assisting disabled persons. Most automation activities that result in machine-readable data files have been created for management efficiency or to cut down on duplicate work efforts.

On-line systems can provide libraries with information in computer-readable form, which can be translated into (1) large-screen, big-text presentations for the visually impaired; (2) speech output of displays, so that disabled persons can hear the results of a search (and record them on a cassette recorder); or (3) Braille output on tape.

Since hearing-impaired or deaf patrons or workers can usually read the CRT screen, machine-readable data files are instantly useful to them. Increasing the size of what is displayed on the screen through video systems or projection devices is the simplest accommodation for visually disabled persons. Over the last year, a number of companies have developed plasma display devices for computer-screen displays that make use of the overhead projector. A small tablet device is attached to the computer output and placed on the overhead projector. Whatever is displayed on the screen will also appear on the plasma display of the tablet. Light shining through the plasma display will then project the images onto a screen or wall. Prices range from $800 to $1,200. Chapter 6 discusses public-services use of such devices.

Appendix C provides a list of vendors (with addresses and telephone numbers) who can supply various communication and adaptive devices, peripherals, and software, so that disabled persons can utilize computer-related library materials more effectively. There are attachment devices to convert computer output to speech or Braille (see Chapter 2).

As libraries begin to select reference tools on CD/ROM such as *Books in Print,* the various H. W. Wilson indexes, PAIS, and other indexing services, the ability of disabled persons to utilize reference tools is enhanced. The same principle applies when libraries acquire the capacity to display the full text of journal articles on the screen and store that text in a local data base. Information Access Corporation now offers *Magazine Index* together with microform full text of the periodical, indexed in addition to *Magazines A.S.A.P.* on-line.

The use of computer-readable resources by the disabled will occur only if the library staff thinks about this particular use during the selection process. Questions that need to be asked include

- If we have this resource in machine-readable form, where shall we place the equipment to provide the best access?

- What special equipment or peripherals do we need to allow disabled persons to use this resource?

- Does this additional equipment create noise problems for other patrons? (Do not assume that the output of speech synthesis machines is comforting to the ear. If there are problems, special "output" areas may need to be considered.)

- Are there copyright-infringement problems involved in the particular use suggested, and if so, can we seek specific, limited permission for disabled users?

- Will use by disabled persons and nondisabled persons create queues not experienced with previous use patterns?

Creating new opportunities may mean that people will have to wait. Under the principle of least effort, the library staff should be prepared for the acquisition of additional resources and/or equipment.

CONCLUSION

In this chapter the selection process has been discussed in terms of selection of materials *about* disabling conditions and disabled persons and selection of materials *for* disabled persons. The next issue facing the library staff will be what to do with the materials selected. How are the materials to be organized, and what forms of access to those materials are going to be created?

REFERENCES

Apple Computer, Inc. 1987. *Resources in special education and rehabilitation.* 3 vols. Cupertino, CA: Apple Computer, Inc. (in association with the Trace Research and Development Center and the assistance of Closing the Gap).

Baskin, B. H., and Harris, K. H. 1977. *Notes from a different drummer: A guide to juvenile fiction portraying the handicapped.* New York: Bowker.

_____. 1984. *More notes from a different drummer: A guide to juvenile fiction portraying the disabled.* New York: Bowker.

Biklen, D., and Bogdan, R. 1977. Media portrayals of disabled people: A study in stereotypes. *Interracial Books for Children Bulletin* 8(6, 7).

Bopp, R. E. 1980. Periodicals for the disabled: Their importance as information sources. *Serials Librarian* 5(2), 61–70.

Friedberg, J. B., Mullins, J. B., and Sukiennik, A. W. 1985. *Accept me as I am: Best books of juvenile nonfiction on impairments and disabilities.* New York: Bowker.

Gibson, M. 1981. *Building a library collection on blindness and handicaps: Basic materials and resources.* Washington, DC: National Library Service for the Blind and Physically Handicapped.

Glimps, B. E. 1983. Books can make mainstreaming easier. *PTA today* 8(60), 23–24.

Lass, B., and Bromfield, M. 1981. Books about children with special needs: An annotated bibliography. *Reading Teacher* 34(5), 530–538.

The National Center on Educational Media and Materials for the Handicapped. 1977. *Guidelines for the Representation of Exceptional Persons in Educational Materials.* Cleveland: The Center.

The National Easter Seal Society. n.d. *Portraying persons with disabilities in print.* Chicago: The Society, 2023 West Ogden Ave., Chicago, IL 60612.

National Library Service for the Blind and Physically Handicapped. 1983. Bibliography: Library Services for the blind and physically handicapped in the United States. In *That all may read: Library service for blind and physically handicapped people.* Washington, DC: Author, 431–506.

_____. 1984. *National organizations concerned with visually and handicapped persons.* Washington, DC: National Library Service.

Offerman, M. C. 1984. The handicapped person: A bibliography. *Catholic Library World* 55(7), 287–289.

President's Committee on the Employment of the Handicapped. 1982. *Rehabilitation for independent living.* Edited by Lois O. Schwab. Washington, DC: The Committee.

Radencich, M. C. 1986. Literature for children and adolescents about people who happen to have a handicap. *Techniques* 2(4), 364–369.

Ralph, J. B. 1982. A geriatric visual concern: The need for publishing guidelines. *Journal of the American Optometric Association,* 43–50.

Schwartz, A. V. 1977. Disability in children's books: Is visibility enough? *Interracial Books for Children Bulletin* 8(6,7).

Tinker, M. A. 1963. *Legibility of Print.* Ames, IA: Iowa State University Press.

United Nations Division for Economic and Social Information. 1985. *Improving communications about people with disabilities.* New York: Division, Department of Public Information, New York, NY 10017.

An update to "A reader's guide for parents of children with mental, physical or emotional disabilities." 1983. Baltimore: Maryland State Planning Council on Developmental Disabilities.

Velleman, R. A. 1980. Library service to the disabled: an annotated bibliography of journals and newsletters. *Serials Librarian* 5(2), 49–60.

4

Organizing the Library Collection for Accessibility: Integration of Materials, Appropriate Subject Headings, and the Impact of Technology

Once the library staff are committed to serving and working with disabled persons, careful thought should be given to the organization of materials in the collection. If the staff select a variety of materials for disabled persons, the library will have materials in a variety of formats: recordings, large-type books, Braille books. Now the library is faced with the problem of making those materials available and integrating them into the library collection.

INTEGRATING MATERIALS

Davis and Davis (1980) discuss the social implications of display and shelf arrangement of materials. Library staff will need to consider carefully what the library's display communicates. If all nonfiction books in the children's collection are in the children's area, it is not likely that adults with poor reading skills who need information will seek that information in the children's area. If all nonfiction is shelved together, there is more opportunity for people (of whatever reading level) to find the information they need in an appropriate form.

In the same way, acquiring materials for disabled persons and arranging those materials in a special area for the disabled are likely to discourage not only disabled persons but also other people who might need or want large-print or recorded materials. The more the materials are integrated in shelving, the more opportunities people have to find the right materials in the appropriate formats. There are, however, a number of problems:

1. Physically, most libraries house their materials in stack areas. Basic stack design emerged when stacks were "closed" to the public and materials were delivered to the patron. Chapter 5 (on facility accessibility) presents

some details about stack and study area design. To summarize the stack problem: Most stack aisles are too narrow for disabled persons in wheelchairs to use, and the materials are often shelved too high or too low for them to reach. The same problem occurs if library staff arrange displays of "new materials" or categories (mysteries, science fiction) in areas where wheelchairs cannot go or with materials on very low shelves.

2. There are some legal problems with materials from the National Library Service for the Blind and Physically Handicapped and films from the Captioned Film for the Deaf Service. These materials are intended for use with "eligible" or "certified" persons only. The provisions of these regulations are understandable since these "special" copies are intended for an audience that cannot utilize the formats under copyright. When libraries house such materials, care must be taken that their proper use requirements are not violated. None of these provisions apply to materials (recorded or captioned) purchased by the library for use by the general population.

3. Many of the appropriate formats require special equipment for their use. Or the use of print formats by disabled persons requires special sensory-adaptation equipment such as video enlargement systems, Kruzweil-type reading machines. The size of such equipment, the need for electrical outlets (with proper wattage), and the noise of such equipment should all be considered.

4. Library-materials storage facilities were designed when *the* format was print. Shelves are simply not designed to hold a variety of size and formats of materials. School-library media centers have had a great deal of experience with varied formats of materials (kits, charts, study prints, filmstrips, cassettes, video) and have developed some plastic bags for holding items and hanging them on rods in shelf areas. Some library suppliers sell book-type boxes for various media, so that the media format can be shelved like a book. Video cassettes now come in a shelvable box, and the library will often have to consider the costs of creating (or buying) appropriate containers if it wishes to integrate shelving and displays.

These problems are presented here so that library staff can consider them as they plan for the integration of materials for disabled persons with collections. Often, full integration of formats and related equipment is not feasible; yet the goal should be to integrate the collection as much as possible, so that disabled persons are not served in isolation from the general population. Chapter 5 will deal with the problem of access isolation when disabled persons must use separate entrances and special service areas. As Davis and Davis (1980, p. 88) point out, the goal of the library staff should be to increase the variety of uses to which people (including disabled people) put library materials. To use materials, people must have access to them, and the catalog must inform them about what is available.

PROVIDING ACCESS WHEN INTEGRATION IS NOT POSSIBLE

As the number and types of materials increase, libraries face increasing problems in keeping track of the information content of their materials (Salton, 1975, p. 3). Libraries can provide good access to the content of their collections *if* they have subject catalogs that give the patrons appropriate access to that collection.

All library staff are familiar with the process of subject cataloging as practiced in their own library. Increasingly, libraries are not doing original subject cataloging of the materials they acquire but are utilizing some type of cooperative cataloging system (ordering preprinted cards, OCLC, CD/ROM files, CIP) to acquire a bibliographic description. Usually that bibliographic description contains several subject headings and, often, added entries for the particular item. Libraries accept these subject headings and added entries by creating (or buying) unit records of the bibliographic description, adding headings to copies of that description, and filing these cards in a card catalog. This process produces an alphabetical index of authors, titles, and subjects that American librarians have come to call the dictionary catalog.

Using this basic finding tool as a base, library staff can create intellectual access to materials in all parts of the library and, with the addition of location codes, can indicate where certain materials are stored. In addition, information about *format* of materials can be indicated not only in the description of the item but also by color coding on the cards. Some libraries that store items by format also utilize a special prefix on call numbers to indicate type of format and to assist library staff in returning the formatted materials to their proper location.

Card catalogs also present the library staff with major cost problems if they attempt to make local modifications to the bibliographic information they receive about a particular item. If a technical services department simply accepts what is received (from the Library of Congress or elsewhere), headings can quickly be typed on cards and the cards filed. Two problems emerge: (1) what to do when the other agency changes its subject headings or when the "rules" of the cataloging process change (as when AACR II was adopted) and (2) what to do when the language of the society changes, so that currently used terminology reflects attitudes like racism, sexism, and "handicapism."

Since this book is not a text on descriptive or subject cataloging and the rules of cataloging, we will not deal with the question of updating subject headings in response to catalog code or other agency decisions. However, because the subject part of a catalog *informs* the user of that catalog, the second question about stereotypical subject entries will be discussed.

ALTERATION OF STEREOTYPED SUBJECT HEADINGS

Library staff must be concerned about the costs of modification to subject headings. First, there are the actual costs of making the modification and maintaining an authority file of the decisions made in subject-heading modifications. Second, there is the potential that major modifications will make one library's records incompatible with those of other cooperating libraries. In a time of increasing networking among libraries, the need for consistent records combined into one file should be considered.

However, can libraries afford not to deal with stereotyped subject headings? As Davis and Davis (1980, p. 91) put it:

> Traditionally, cataloging goals have included the desire to be objective, ac-curate, and humane. These, of course, are ideals toward which we strive, doing the best we can in light of the values current in our society.
> These goals have a very practical importance. Headings and terms are surrogates for the materials listed in the cataloging. These surrogates shape the seekers who use the catalog even before they reach the material. Subject catalogs predispose people and reinforce assumptions and attitudes.

The words librarians put in subject headings or the subject headings they accept from other sources, *do* influence patrons. Especially in educational settings, the subject catalog and other indexes used in the curriculum do contribute to (or detract from) the educational process. But *every* library is in some sense an educational institution.

Libraries have a history of cultural lag in the subject headings assigned to materials. Berman (1971a, 1971b, 1977a, 1977b, 1984), of the Hennepin County Library system, has been outspoken on the inadequacies and stereotypes of Library of Congress practices in assigning even the minimum number of subject headings they assign (1.3 average according to McClure, 1976). Berman's goal is honest and usable subject access for the user of the library catalog. Under his leadership and that of Elisabeth Dickinson, the Hennepin County Library has established a record of creating and utilizing up-to-date, humane, appropriate subject headings in their system. Foskett (1984) has expressed similar concerns on the international scene. As Likins (1984) has stressed, many Library of Congress subject headings (and sub-divisions) are silly and obviously unclear to any library patron who speaks English as a native language. If a library policy is to copy verbatim what the Library of Congress does ("my national library, right or wrong"), it is hoped that the clientele of that library is much like the clientele of the Library of Congress. Library staff can decide to perpetuate the status quo in the society through the use of subject headings, or they can decide, as part of an overall library strategy of ending discrimination against disabled persons, that they will go to the expense of modifying subject headings to reflect a more enlightened view.

Davis and Davis (1980, pp. 108–154) compare the subject-heading approach of the Library of Congress with *Sears List of Subject Headings,* and add their own suggestions for more adequate and humane subject headings in an extensive list. Several brief examples from the Davises' work are presented in Table 4.1.

TABLE 4.1 Subject-Heading Approaches

HC = Hennepin County; LC = Library of Congress; SE = Sears

DA = authors' suggestions

HC: Architecture and the handicapped
  x Architectural barriers for the handicapped
   Architecture and handicapped persons
   Architecture, barrier-free
   Barrier-free architecture
   Handicapped and architecture
LC: Architecture and the handicapped
  SEE ALSO
   Architecture and handicapped children
   Architecture and the aged
   Architecture and the mentally handicapped
   Architecture and the physically handicapped
DA: Architecture and handicapped persons
   Architecture and disabled persons [preferred]

HC: Handicapped children (*Note:* Make dual entry under Mentally handicapped children or Physically handicapped children.)
  SEE ALSO
   Hyperactive children
  x Children, Disabled
   Children, Handicapped
   Disabled children
LC: Handicapped Children
  SEE ALSO
   Aphasic children
   Architecture and handicapped children
   Brain-damaged children
   Hyperactive children
   Mentally handicapped children
   Perceptually handicapped children
   Physical education for handicapped children
   Physically handicapped children
   Socially handicapped children
  x Abnormal children
   Children, Abnormal and backward
 xx Child study
   Exceptional children

SE: Handicapped children
   SEE ALSO
   Hyperactive children
   Mentally handicapped children
   Physically handicapped children
   Socially handicapped children
  x Abnormal children
   Children, Abnormal
 xx Exceptional children
DA: Disabled children [preferred]
   [Drop x Abnormal children; Children, Abnormal; and Children, Abnormal
   and backward (they are offensive terms).]

Library staff may wish to consult the Hennepin County Public Library (1984) policy and the *HCL Cataloging Bulletins* from that library for other suggestions.

PRINCIPLES FOR BETTER SUBJECT HEADINGS

The same basic principles apply to the language of subject headings as apply to selecting materials for the library (see Chapter 3). Feelings have run so high about the topic of prejudicial subject headings that the Resources and Technical Services Division of the American Library Association established an ad hoc committee on racism and sexism in subject analysis (RTSD, 1981).

Marshall (1977, p. 6) defines the hypothetical user of the Library of Congress subject headings:

> The reader has been identified as American/Western European, Christian, white, heterosexual, and male. The identification is not surprising since it reflects the point of view that has been dominant for so long in our society. But that point of view does not accurately reflect the world we live in. Non-Americans/Western Europeans, non–Christians, non-white, non-heterosexuals, and non-males exist in numbers and have always existed in numbers....
>
> Ideals aside, one fact remains. The attempt to identify a single reader, and therefore the creation of a hypothetical norm, has resulted in subject descriptors which serve some and disserve or underserve the many.

The authors of this book would only add to her list: disabled persons. Marshall (pp. 6–10) goes on to identify "principles for establishing subject headings relating to people and peoples."

1. Establish (if possible) the authentic name of ethnic, national, religious, social, sexual (and disabled person) groups. Cite the authority in a subject-heading authority list. If no authentic name can be found, use the name preferred by the specific group. The literature of the people should be

the basis for decision. Have your disabled staff and patrons assist in selecting headings. For example, how do disabled persons refer to themselves in their national organization's publications? Do they prefer *handicapped, disabled,* or other terms to describe their situation? Do groups use technical or medical terms to refer to specific disabilities, or do they use more common terms?

2. When subdivisions are established, the connotation of words should be considered. Avoid words that connote inferiority or perculiarity. Use neutral words. When in doubt, consult with members of specific disability groups about current accepted terminology.

3. Wording and structure of headings for majority and minority groups should be the same. Avoid *as* and *in* in building headings (e.g., group *as* criminals, or group *in* activity).

4. Be specific and current. Do not stretch older terms to cover new topics. When in doubt, make two specific entries. Groups and nations change their names. A member of the technical-services staff should be assigned the task of keeping up-to-date about terminology used in rehabilitation, special education, and the publications of disabled persons.

5. Avoid subsuming terminology (*Pilgrim Fathers* for all the *Pilgrims*) and establishing headings for some groups and not others (if there is an activity for women, there is also likely to be a literature on the activity for men and for the disabled).

6. Do not build huge files under some undifferentiated heading. As the collection grows, subject headings need to be made more specific to aid the users in searching. Cross-references need to be changed to refer users to more specific headings from general headings in the catalog. Very large subject areas should have a "scope note" that instructs users to seek more specific headings and gives examples:

Disabled Persons
SCOPE NOTE:
Used for general descriptions of persons with disabilities. More specific information will be found under specific disabling conditions; e.g., Physically disabled persons, Hearing-impaired persons, etc.

Basic principles for building appropriate subject headings related to disabled persons can be summed up in a very few words: Be sensitive to the connotations of language; avoid thinking from the perspective of white, English-speaking, nondisabled males; and seek out literature related to your collection and its users that can be used to authenticate terminology of headings. The library technical-services staff that already employ disabled persons in paraprofessional and professional positions will be in the best position to carry out this task.

ACCESS TO ON-LINE CATALOGS

Many libraries are converting their standard finding tool, the card catalog, to some form of machine-readable file. As prices for hardware and software have decreased, the possibilities for on-line catalogs and circulation systems have become more and more attractive to libraries. Even small libraries and school-library media centers can now consider interactive circulation systems with bar codes and simple subject category, title, author, and call-number access.

Practically speaking, when a library materials' bibliographic records are in machine-readable form, a number of options become available to the library technical-services staff.

First, the library staff can consider the costs and benefits of having their authority file on-line as a part of the total system. The ability to review the authority file *while* working on the assignment of subject headings and cross-references increases the possibility of consistent, appropriate headings and cross-references. The addition of comprehensive "catalogers' notes" to that file will greatly aid the process of training new technical-services personnel. Making the authority file part of the on-line system will also make some cataloging staff position potentially available to disabled persons, since awkward loose-leaf, card, or bound authority files will not have to be manipulated. Also, if the authority file is in machine-readable format, it can be enlarged on the screen of a monitor or converted to Braille or voice output with adaptive aids. See Appendixes B and C for a list of information sources and vendors of such aids.

As microcomputers become more powerful in accessible "on-board" memory, such computers can be used with dual "windows" that provide a display of the item currently being worked on and a display of the authority file. Thus the technical-services staff can view the authority file *at the same time* as the particular bibliographic record and edit that record appropriately.

Second, the library staff can investigate the possibilities of regularly updating their authority file and correcting the main file as a part of that operation. The main arguments for not correcting out-of-date and inappropriate subject headings have always had to do with the work required to change the headings on "all those cards." Librarians spent a great deal of money on electric erasers and specially colored "liquid paper" in attempting to keep up with the necessary changes in Dewey schedules and subject headings. Another cost, not always visible to the catalog user, was the cost of changing cross-reference structure in the catalog, so that people would not be referred from one heading to another heading where there was no information ("blind" cross-references). Keeping the syndetic structure of the catalog sensible took time and money.

Machine-readable records and authority files do not solve all of the intellectual problems of syndetic structure in subject access; however, the costs of changing specific headings and cross-references in the main subject catalog can now be accomplished very economically by utilizing the "search and replace" function available in most system editors. A task that once required pulling all subject cards and all cards used in cross-references now becomes a task of defining the "old" term and replacing it with the "new" term throughout the file. Editing of the authority file is also easier utilizing this search-replace function. Ease of editing and utilizing the authority file should be one criteron for selection in purchasing an on-line catalog system.

It is possible to develop a computer program for authority-file maintenance that will automatically produce the traditional "opposites" of syndetic structure, so that when a "SEE" reference is created, the "X" reference is also created, and when a "SEE ALSO" reference is created, an "XX" reference is created. This type of programming, when combined with a program segment that takes multiple word headings and rotates them for filing on each significant word, makes the editing of the authority file for syndetic logic much easier since contradictions show up in the sorted file and are easily removed. Such programs allow the technical-services staff to enter

Abnormal Children   SEE   Handicapped Children

and automatically create the reverse entry:

Handicapped Children   X   Abnormal Children

as well as these entries:

Children, Abnormal   SEE   Handicapped Children
Children, Handicapped   SEE   Handicapped Children

Keeping the authority file up-to-date is essential to keeping the on-line subject-access file (or the microfiche catalog) useful to library patrons. The up-to-date authority file is also essential to the assignment of appropriate subject headings by the technical-services staff. Anderson (1988) describes a data-base creation-and-maintenance program at Rutgers University that provides a wide array of authority-file (thesaurus) functions to librarians.

Third, once the bibliographic records are in machine-readable form, the library staff can consider various ways of displaying that information on terminal or microcomputer monitors. Traditionally, the CRT screen has been treated like the page of a book in libraries; screens are filled with text, usually in one type size, for the patron to read. However, computer displays can be modified by programs so that text is displayed in larger (or smaller) characters and in a variety of foreground and background colors utilizing a good color monitor. These modifications should not require major reprogramming of the system. However, some turnkey systems do not allow modifications in the screen-map section of the program without major program adjustments. Library staff evaluating the purchase of a system should critically review the displayed output of the computer for each different screen of information the patron will see. Some specific questions can be asked:

- Can this display be enlarged without losing information?
- Does the display indicate important words or messages by highlighting the particular words or using flashing display (or a different color)?
- Does the text of the display make sense? (Remember that a reading-level test of one display revealed that the reading level required a college degree!) The display should make sense to its intended users, not just the library staff.
- What modifications can be made in the display of text screens and layout of pages? Sometimes modifications can be made only by the vendor of the system *at its facility*.

Fourth and finally, library staff should consider the expense and convenience of having at least one display unit for the on-line catalog system that can be used to convert screen-text displays to formats appropriate for disabled users. These will include the ability of the computer to translate text on the screen, utilizing a speech synthesizer, so that the screen display is "spoken" to the patron or screen output that can be "printed out" on a Braille machine (paper or paperless type). (See Chapter 2 for suggestions on this topic.)

POSSIBILITIES FOR THE SMALL LIBRARY
OR MEDIA CENTER

Probably small libraries will not automate their card catalogs into public-access on-line systems unless they are part of a regional library system or a centralized catalog system within a school district. Every library, no matter what size, can utilize a microcomputer and word-processing or database software to create bibliographies, lists, and other finding aids for its patrons. Such finding aids should be written in currently acceptable vocabulary. Offensive (sexist, racist, and disabled-ist) vocabulary should be eliminated from the card catalog by creating appropriate SEE references and at least changing the subject headings to more appropriate entries. Vertical-file subject headings should be evaluated in terms of their vocabulary, and changes should be made to agree with the modifications in the subject-heading list. A small library can easily maintain a subject-authority file with cataloger's notes and cross-references in a word-processing file utilizing a microcomputer. Almost every microcomputer company now has simple, inexpensive voice synthesizers for its equipment that can be used to "speakout" bibliographies or lists for the visually disabled. See the listing of information and vendors in Appendixes B and C.

CONCLUSION

It is obviously cheaper to continue maintaining library catalogs and other finding aids as in the past. Libraries that take seriously the educational impact of their finding tools will want to review the process of creating subject entries and maintaining the cross-reference structure of the catalog. As more and more finding-tool information is modified into machine-readable records on data bases, the possibilities for creating additional up-to-date headings, better cross-references, and more informative displays can be economically explored.

REFERENCES

Anderson, J. D. 1988. Information organization based on textual analysis (IOTA): Instructional Programs for Database Design. In Hannigan, J. A., and Intner, S. S., *The library microcomputer environment*. Phoenix, AZ: Oryx Press, 145–167.

Berman, S. 1971a. Children, "Idiots," the "Underground," and others. *Library Journal* 96, 4162–4167.

———. 1971b. *Prejudice and antipathies: A tract on the Library of Congress subject heads concerning people*. Metuchen, NJ: Scarecrow Press.

———. 1977a. Nitty-gritty heads: A selection of people-helping descriptors LC hasn't gotten around to yet, and a nifty idea to expand the usefulness of your catalog by reference to outside information sources. *Unabashed Librarian* 22, 8.

———. 1977b. Kid's stuff: a grabbag of Hennepin County Library subject headings for (mostly) children's media. *Unabashed Librarian* 25, 6–7.

———. 1981. *The joys of cataloging: Essays, letters, reviews and other explosions*. Phoenix: Oryx Press.

———. 1982. Do-it-yourself Subject Cataloging: Sources and Tools. *Library Journal* 107, 785–786.

———. 1984. *Subject cataloging: Critiques and innovations*. New York: Haworth Press.

Davis, E. A., and Davis, C. M. 1980. Processing and display. *Mainstreaming library service for disabled people*, 83–88.

Dehart, F., and Searles, E. 1985. Developmental values as catalog access points for children's fiction. *Technicalities* 5, 13–15.

Foskett, A. C. 1984. Better dead than read: Further studies in critical classification. *Library Resources and Technical Services* 28, 346–359.

Hennepin County Public Library. 1984. Cataloging and classification policy. *Unabashed Librarian* 50, 19–20.

Likins, J. R. 1984. Subject headings, silly, American — 20th Century — Complications and Sequelae — Addresses, Essays, Lectures. *TSQ 2* 1/2, 3–11.

McClure, C. R. 1976. Subject and added entries as access to information. *Journal of Academic Librarianship* 2, 9–14.

Marshall, J.K. 1977. *On equal terms: A thesaurus for nonsexist indexing and cataloging.* New York: Neal-Schuman Publishers.

Resources and Technical Services Division (1981). Subject analysis: Summary report of the racism and sexism in subject analysis subcommittee to the RTSD/CCS subject analysis committee. *RTSD Newsletter* 6, 21–22.

Salton, G. 1975. Introducing the new library. In *Dynamic information and library processing.* Englewood Cliffs, NJ: Prentice-Hall, 3–38.

5

Making the Library Facilities Accessible

General guidelines are presented for making library facilities and services accessible to disabled persons. Many accessibility features are illustrated. Accessibility of areas outside the building, the building itself, and the interior areas of the library are discussed. Sources of technical information on accessibility modifications are listed. An Accessibility Checklist developed by the Iowa Chapter of the American Institute of Architects concludes the chapter.

THE MAJOR OBSTACLES TO ACCESSIBILITY

Strangely enough, the major obstacle to creating accessible facilities and services is not money or physical barriers. The greatest obstacle is attitudes. Many commonly held attitudes are incorporated into society's mythology about disabled persons and their needs. The Eastern Paralyzed Veterans Association (n.d.) has compiled a listing of currently held myths that create obstacles to accessibility. These myths and the facts related to each are listed below:

1. *The Myth:* Buildings and transportation in the United States are accessible to and usable by persons with disabilities.
   The Facts: Standards related to making facilities accessible emerged in the 1960s and apply only to new construction. Section 504 of the Rehabilitation Act of 1973 requires provision of accessibility, but the large majority of facilities are older and remain inaccessible.
2. *The Myth:* Making facilities usable for disabled persons is expensive.
   The Facts: Extensive surveys show that costs for accessibility in

new construction are only 1 percent of the total (Schroeder and Steinfeld, 1979). Even modifications to existing facilities can be as low as 2 percent of the adjusted original cost of the facility. Given the general aging of our population, most Americans will require some form of access accommodation in both facilities and transportation.

3. *The Myth:* Every square inch of a facility must be accessible.

The Facts: Regulations require that a *reasonable* number of accessible specific building elements should exist, including (1) at least one entrance wide enough for a wheelchair to pass (32 inches), (2) one accessible route of travel to the facility, (3) parking spaces (if there is parking for the public), (4) one accessible elevator (controls 54 inches from the floor), (5) an accessible drinking fountain (54 inches from the floor), (6) one telephone 54 inches from the floor (if public telephones are available), (7) in assembly areas, wheelchair viewing locations, (8) in rest rooms, one fixture of each type, (9) one curb ramp on each side of a pedestrian walk.

4. *The Myth:* There are no funding programs of financial incentives available to provide accessibility.

The Facts: A number of government programs, including the Community Development Block Grants and provisions of the Tax Reform Act of 1984, had provisions designed to encourage accessibility modifications. In October 1986, the income-tax $30,000 tax credit became permanent. Eckstein's *The Handicapped Funding Directory* (latest edition) provides details on various federal, corporate, and foundation grants.

5. *The Myth:* Little technical expertise exists concerning accessibility for disabled persons.

The Facts: Technical information is available from a number of private, professional, and government agencies, with detailed specifications, lists of suppliers, and so on. A list of technical-information sources is included at the end of this chapter.

6. *The Myth:* Making a facility accessible destroys the aesthetic quality of a building.

The Facts: When access is considered during the design of a new building, very pleasing aesthetic perspectives can be added. Ramps are often added to existing buildings and can be made from the same materials as the building facade. A number of design alternatives allow for aesthetic sensibility and the preservation of culturally or historically significant architecture details and style.

Once these myths (or their relatives) have been overcome by the library staff and the library's board of trustees or advisors, the process of accessibility analysis, planning for modifications, and actual accommodations can begin.

DEVELOPING A PLAN FOR ACCESSIBILITY

In developing a plan for accessibility in libraries, the library director and professional staff should remember that accessibility relates to more than the worksite or access to a particular library service. If disabled persons are to use the library or work in the library providing services, they must be able to get to the library, move from the outside of the facility to the inside of the building, and have access to areas of work or service.

This broader perspective on accessibility is essential if the library is to become a place of service and work for disabled persons. Even the most accessible building or worksite can be frustrated because of a curb in the parking lot or lack of public transportation to an accessible location near the library. Library directors and professional staff may wish to study the accessibility of buildings, facilities, and work areas, using the Architectural Checklist (Iowa Chapter, American Institute of Architects, 1974) included at the end of this chapter. This checklist will provide the library staff with necessary information on barriers to access. It is important actually to complete this checklist *at the places named,* not in an office or at a meeting. Take a yardstick or tape measure along to measure various things. Do not depend on memory!

Perhaps the easiest way to start is outside of the library facility. How do people now get to the library? If they drive to the library facility, are there marked parking spaces for the handicapped? Most states now have laws requiring such parking spaces and signs. The parking space itself should be examined to see if there are any barriers between the parking space and an entrance to the library building. Good 12-foot-wide parking spaces do not in themselves create access. Ask the following questions:

- How far is it to the nearest curb cut?
- On which side of the car is the curb cut?
- Is the parking space arranged so that access to an entrance or ramp is nearby?

An ideal arrangement for parking combines the 12-foot-wide parking space (well marked) with access on the same level as the parking area. Sometimes this can be created by having special parking places designated near a front entrance.

Not everyone comes to the library by car. In some urban areas, access by walking and public transportation is possible. If people tend to walk to the library and use public transportation, it is important to determine how accessible the general transportation system is. Ask these questions:

- Can people using wheelchairs or three-wheel scooters go from nearby buildings to and from the library?

- Does the public transportation service provide accessible transportation services (kneeling buses, special elevators in subways, special buses on call)?
- Are traffic signals near the library equipped to provide information to visually impaired and blind persons?

Given the history of public facilities and transportation, the library staff should not be surprised to find that general neighborhood access is limited and public transportation only remotely accessible. Most states now have laws about curb cuts (Eastern Paralyzed Veterans, 1984) and other access to transportation items; however, much remains to be done.

If the area and transportation are generally inaccessible, it may be a waste of time to make the library facility itself more accessible. Consideration should be given to what library services and positions can be moved to accessible locations in the library system. Of course, the long-term solution to access is to make the area (or the city) accessible, and library staff will want to become active in advocating better access and the necessary state and local funding to create that access.

SOURCES OF INFORMATION ON MODIFICATIONS AND EQUIPMENT

A number of sources of information, advice, and equipment are available. A longtime advocate of accommodations for access, Ronald I. Mace, has collected a loose-leaf system of accessible design information. His *The System: Accessible Design and Product Information* (1985) provides an excellent source of accessibility guidelines and *affordable* commercial sources of products to make buildings and work areas accessible. This indexed list of products comes in a three-volume loose-leaf set with regular updates.

Each May, *American School and University* (401 N. Broad Street, Philadelphia, PA 19108) publishes an annual directory of school supplies and equipment, including equipment for assisting disabled students in gaining access to facilities. The U.S. Architectural and Transportation Barriers Compliance Board (Washington, DC 20202) issues pamphlets related to specific equipment and accommodation devices. Recently it has produced *Assistive Listening Systems* and *Using TDDs in Federal Government Communications*. It also has a computerized data base on lifts and wheelchair securements for use in buses and other vehicles. A list of its publications can be obtained from the Public Information Office, 330 C. Street, SW, Washington, DC 20202 (202-245-1591).

The American Coalition of Citizens with Disabilities (1200 15th Street, NW, Suite 201, Washington, DC 20005 (202-785-4265) has information on grass-roots organizations interested in and knowledgeable about access.

Other sources of information:

National Library of Canada. 1987. *The accessible Canadian library: A planning workbook for a barrier free environment.* Ottawa: Canadian Government Publishing Centre.

Offers practical, step-by-step advice on meeting the Canadian goal of all publicly supported libraries becoming barrier-free during the "Decade of Disabled Persons."

National Library Service for the Blind and Physically Handicapped. 1981. *Planning barrier free libraries: A guide for renovation and construction of libraries serving blind and physically handicapped readers.* Washington, DC: The National Library Service.

Provides an illustrated planning guide to new-building construction or building renovation. The guide covers all library-staff and public-operations areas.

Velleman, R. A. 1981. Architectural and program accessibility: A review of library programs. *Drexel Library Quarterly* 16(2), 32–47.

Describes legislation and building-design criteria related to accessibility and includes a bibliography of sources for further information.

THE BASIC FEATURES OF ACCESSIBILITY

Parking Spaces

Spaces should be on the same level as the main entrance of the library and should be clearly marked with the international sign for handicapped access. Each parking place should be at least 12 feet wide and provide open access on one side of the car. When parking cannot be provided on the same level as the main entrance, it should be provided in the general parking area as near the building as possible, with curb cuts and ramps so that an entrance is accessible by wheelchair.

The building and its entrances should be easily accessible, with ramps and spring-loaded doors that can be opened by disabled persons. Access walks should be smooth and hard-surfaced. Where possible, access routes for disabled persons should be the same as those for other persons; people who work together should be able to enter the building together.

Figure 5.1 illustrates some of these characteristics in a typical building situation.

Interiors

Interior halls, access routes in work areas, doorways, and work areas should be able to accommodate persons using crutches or wheelchairs or with limited use of their arms. The space to negotiate a wheelchair is often overlooked by those who have never used one. A wheelchair seen from the side has the dimensions shown in Figure 5.2.

FIGURE 5.1   Facility and Ramp Access

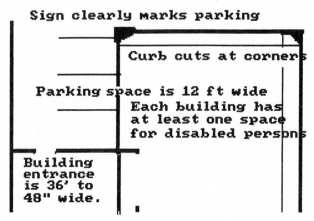

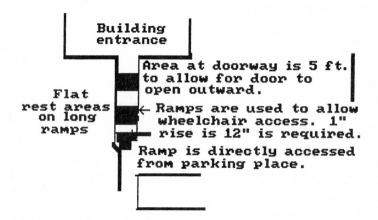

FIGURE 5.2   Wheelchair Dimensions

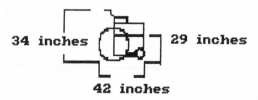

The size of the wheelchair (including the footrests) means that its turning area is about 6 feet square. Skilled operators can get by with a smaller space by moving back and forward a number of times; operators of electric-powered chairs may need slightly more space. The small front wheels on the wheelchair also present problems when the floor has abrupt changes in level or when there is loose carpet. Interior floor coverings should be nonslip surfaces, so that individuals using crutches or braces can travel safely. If carpets are installed, they should be hard piles on a rubber backing, so that wheelchairs and crutches do not get caught. If a book truck will operate on the carpet efficiently, so will a wheelchair. While carpet is pleasing to the eye and restful to the feet, the number of library operations requiring movement on wheeled vehicles should long ago have eliminated all carpet that does not take wheeled vehicles easily. Turning space and obstacles to wheelchair access are illustrated in Figure 5.3.

FIGURE 5.3 Wheelchair Operation

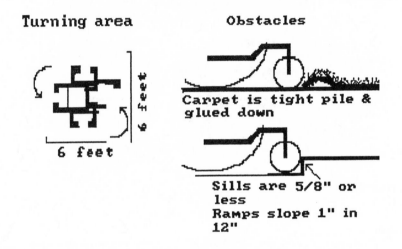

Turning area

6 feet

Obstacles

Carpet is tight pile & glued down

Sills are 5/8" or less
Ramps slope 1" in 12"

Entrances and Doorways

Building entrances (exits) and interior doorways need careful evaluation for wheelchair access. The opening of the door must be between 28 and 36 inches. Do not measure the doorway from frame to frame but from one frame to the part of the door that projects into the doorway; this measurement is the true opening. The only doors that can be fully opened are doors that slide into the wall, and these doors are not manually operable by persons in wheelchairs. The space around doors is also critical. Disabled persons in wheelchairs will need an area on either side of the door to get the door open, getting through the door and past the door, so that it can be closed. A five-square-feet level and clear area is recommended. If the door is near a corner, be sure that there is some access for the person in a wheelchair. Hardware for doors should be modified so that a disabled person can easily open the door. Electrically operated doors may be a good solution, provided that the door does not abruptly swing *toward* the person seeking entrance. There are a number of lever door openers as well as push-bar lever openers for doors. Remember that door handles are difficult for persons with packages, older persons, and those whose reach is limited by temporary injury. Replacement of door hardware will be of benefit to many workers and patrons.

An illustration of doorway accommodations appears in Figure 5.4.

FIGURE 5.4.   Entrance Access

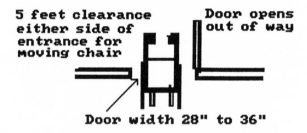

If door opens toward
person, space is needed
for backing wheelchair

5 feet clearance   Door opens
either side of   out of way
entrance for
moving chair

Door width 28" to 36"

Obstacles

Fire extinguishers, fountains, and signs should be located so that they do not become obstacles for visually impaired workers or patrons. In the same way, furniture should not be rearranged without informing visually impaired and blind workers who have memorized locations of items, so that they can continue to move about easily. See Figure 5.5.

FIGURE 5.5   Obstacles to Access

Low overhanging signs,
fire extinguishers,
fountains, and other
protruding objects can be
hazardous to blind and
visually impaired person

Mark or remove obstacles

Personal Areas

Areas such as bathrooms, drinking fountains, snack bars, drink machines, microwave ovens, and light switches should be accessible to persons using wheelchairs, crutches, or other mobility devices. Mirrors should be tilted so that they are usable, handles of faucets modified for easy use. Some of these accommodations are illustrated in Figure 5.6.

FIGURE 5.6 Bathroom and Toilet Modifications

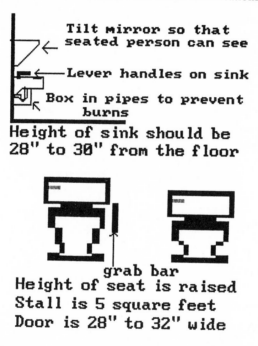

Tilt mirror so that seated person can see

Lever handles on sink

Box in pipes to prevent burns

Height of sink should be 28" to 30" from the floor

grab bar

Height of seat is raised

Stall is 5 square feet

Door is 28" to 32" wide

Work Areas, Stacks

Worktables, desks, and so on may need to be raised to allow for wheelchair access. The height of worktables is typically too low to allow for a wheelchair so that the individual's knees are under the table. Minimum height is about 28 inches. Tables should not have barriers underneath ("aprons") that prevent access. A person in a wheelchair has a reach of about 30 inches, which means that books, computer terminals, and other tools must be within that range. In carrels, equipment controls must be accessible without strain, and the carrel must have an opening width of 32 inches. If the carrel is too narrow, it is inaccessible (even if high enough). Some workers may require a table or work desk at standing height during part of the day as physical therapy.

In bookstack areas, the aisles should be at least 36 inches wide to allow for access by persons using crutches and wheelchairs. Library bookstacks are often a problem because basic stack design was determined during a period when all library stacks were closed to patrons. The assumption was that when a patron wanted materials, the nondisabled library page would go into the stacks, find the materials, and bring them to the patron at the circulation desk. Many older stacks are therefore very close together, immovable, and very high.

The person in a wheelchair is limited in reaching up to about 50 inches and in reaching down to about 20 inches. Within this range, many disabled persons in wheelchairs can use the stacks (if they can get into them). Obviously, libraries cannot afford fully accessible bookstacks. However, the library should develop a plan to make all library materials accessible to workers and patrons. This plan will often include making certain high-use materials available in accessible stacks, on acccessible tables. It may also include the conversion of some high-use materials to either microform (available at an accessible reader-printer) or CD/ROM format for certain indexes, encyclopedias, news services, and technical materials. As more and more materials become available in machine-readable formats, some of the access problems will be overcome if libraries make microcomputers or terminals accessible to disabled persons. Some materials will continue to require delivery from the stacks to the worker or patron. Carrel and stack access is illustrated in Figure 5.7.

FIGURE 5.7   Carrel and Stack Access

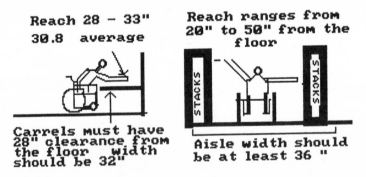

Reach 28 – 33"
30.8 average

Reach ranges from 20" to 50" from the floor

Carrels must have 28" clearance from the floor width should be 32"

Aisle width should be at least 36 "

Communications

Telephones and intercom systems may need relocation or modification for use by disabled persons. Speaker phones are often useful in this context. Variable-volume-control telephones and Telecommunication Devices for the Deaf (TDDs) may also be needed. A variety of TDD devices are available for office, home, and travel use.

Signs

Sign systems should all include areas of Braille markings or raised lettering. Any maps of facilities should be marked so that visually impaired and blind persons can use them. Where sign systems involve sound as a signal, as in fire or exit alarms, the system should include flashing lights to alert the hearing-impaired and deaf worker or patron. Kamisar's *Signs for the Handicapped Patron* (1979) is a helpful resource when evaluating sign systems.

SOURCES OF TECHNICAL INFORMATION

Most states have building regulations for *new* construction of facilities and transportation. The following list of governmental and professional sources will provide a beginning for acquiring technical-facility design information.

American National Standards Institute. 1980. *Specification for making buildings and facilities accessible to, and usable by, physically handicapped people.* New York: The Institute.
  The standard to which all other standards are compared.
Architectural and Transportation Barriers Compliance Board. 1981. *Minimum guidelines and requirements for accessible design.* Washington, DC: The Board.
———. n.d. *Resource guide to literature on a barrier-free environment.* Washington, DC: The Board.
  Fifteen-hundred-entry bibliography on research studies, legislation, etc.
Department of Housing and Urban Development. 1977. *Barrier free site design.* Washington, DC: The Department.
  Older but useful publication with good illustrations and an extensive bibliography.
Eastern Paralyzed Veterans Association. n.d. *Building design requirements for the physically handicapped.* rev. ed. New York: The Association.
  Brief descriptions with excellent drawings to exact scale of the provisions of the building codes of New York, New Jersey, Pennsylvania, and Connecticut.
———. 1984. *Curbcuts: How to design and construct proper curb cuts in Connecticut, New Jersey, New York and Pennsylvania.* New York: The Association.
General Services Administration. 1985. *Uniform federal accessibility standards.* Washington, DC: The Administration, Department of Defense, Department of Housing and Urban Development, United States Postal Service. (Originally published in the *Federal Register* for August 7, 1984.)
  Presents uniform standards for the design, construction, and alteration of buildings, so that physically handicapped persons will have ready access. Based on the Architectural Barriers Act, 42 U.S.C. secs. 4151–4157.
Mace, R. L., and Laslett, B. 1977. *An illustrated handbook of the handicapped section of the North Carolina Building Code.* Raleigh, NC: North Carolina Department of Insurance.

An illustrated guide to the provisions of the North Carolina Building Code.
Each part of the code is presented, then illustrated graphically and with text.

CONCLUSION

The process of staff selection and training, materials selection and
organization, as well as the programs and services of the library designed
to include disabled persons, can be frustrated by the fact that disabled persons are not able to get to, enter, and use the library facility. This chapter
has outlined some of the basic concepts in facility accessibility. Not every
library will be able to afford total facility accessibility; however, all libraries
can evaluate their facility's accessibility and make plans to provide access
in as many areas as possible by facility modifications or moving programs
and services to accessible locations. Every library should have a long-range
accessibility plan, so that when the facility is renovated or a new facility is
constructed, it can be made fully accessible. (See the Accessibility Checklist
that follows.)

SUGGESTED ACCESSIBILITY COMPLIANCE CHECKLIST

A. PARKING LOTS

	YES	NO
1. Are accessible spaces approximate to the facility?	___	___
Are they identified with appropriate signs?	___	___
2. Are there parking spaces open on one side, allowing 12		
feet minimum width for individuals in wheelchairs or on		
braces and crutches to get in and out onto a level surface?	___	___
3. Is it unnecessary for individuals in wheelchairs or those		
using braces or crutches to wheel or walk behind parked		
cars?	___	___
4. Is distribution of spaces for use by disabled persons in ac-		
cord with frequency and persistence of parking needs?	___	___

COMMENTS: _____

_____

B. WALKS

	YES	NO
1. Are public walks at least 48 inches wide?	___	___
Is the gradient not greater than 5 percent?	___	___
2. Are walks of a continuing common surface not inter-		
rupted by steps or abrupt changes of level?	___	___
3. Wherever they cross other walks, driveways, or parking		
lots, do walks blend to a common level?	___	___

YES   NO

4. Do walks have a level platform at the top which is (a) at least 5 feet by 5 feet if a door swings out onto the platform or toward the walk or (b) 3 feet by 5 feet if the door does not swing onto the platform?   ___   ___

5. Does the platform extend at least one foot beyond each side of the door?   ___   ___

COMMENTS: _____

C. RAMPS

YES   NO

1. Do ramps have a slope no greater than 1 foot rise in 12 feet?

2. Do ramps have a handrail on at least one side?   ___   ___
   Are they 32 inches in height from ramp surface?   ___   ___
   Are surfaces smooth?
   Do they extend 1 foot beyond the top & bottom of the ramp?   ___   ___

3. Do ramps have a nonslip surface?   ___   ___

4. Do ramps have at least 6 feet of straight clearance at the bottom?   ___   ___

5. Do ramps have level platforms at 30 foot intervals and wherever they turn?   ___   ___

COMMENTS: _____

D. ENTRANCES/EXITS

YES   NO

1. Is at least one primary entrance to each building usable by individuals in wheelchairs? (It is preferable that all or most entrances/exits should be accessible to disabled persons.)   ___   ___

2. Is at least one entrance usable by individuals in wheelchairs on a level that would make elevators accessible?   ___   ___

COMMENTS: _____

E. DOORS AND DOORWAYS

YES   NO

1. Do doors have a clear opening of no less than 32 inches?   ___   ___
   Are they operable by a single effort? (Note: Two-leaf doors are not usable by disabled persons unless one of the two leaves is 32 inches wide.)   ___   ___

2. Are the doors operable with pressure or strength that could reasonably be expected from disabled persons?   ___   ___

3. Is the floor on the inside or the outside of each doorway level for a distance of 5 feet from the door in the direction of door swing?   ___   ___
   Does the floor extend 1 foot beyond each side of the door?   ___   ___

Compliance Checklist, cont.   YES   NO

4. Are sharp inclines and abrupt changes in level avoided at doorsills?   ____   ____
5. Do door closers allow the use of the door by disabled persons?   ____   ____

COMMENTS: _____

F. STAIRS AND STEPS

                                            YES   NO

1. Do steps avoid abrupt nosing?   ____   ____
2. Do stairs have handrails 32 inches high, measured from the tread at the face of the riser?   ____   ____
3. Do stairs have at least one handrail that extends at least 18 inches beyond the top and bottom step?   ____   ____
4. Do steps have risers of 7 inches or less?   ____   ____

COMMENTS: _____

G. FLOORS

                                            YES   NO

1. Do floors have a nonslip surface?   ____   ____
2. Are floors on each story at a common level or connected by a ramp?   ____   ____

COMMENTS: _____

H. REST ROOMS

                                            YES   NO

1. Is there an appropriate number of rest rooms for each sex?   ____   ____
   Are they accessible to disabled persons?   ____   ____
   Are they usable by disabled persons?   ____   ____
2. Do toilet rooms have turning space of 5 feet by 5 feet to allow traffic of individuals in wheelchairs?   ____   ____
3. Do toilet rooms have at least one toilet stall that
   Is three feet wide?   ____   ____
   Is at least 4 feet 8 inches deep? (Prefer 5 feet.)   ____   ____

COMMENTS: _____

I. PUBLIC TELEPHONES

                                            YES   NO

1. Are there an appropriate number of public telephones accessible to disabled persons?   ____   ____
2. Type: Booth_____   Wall Mount_____
3. Is height of dial (or push buttons) 48 inches or less from the floor?   ____   ____
4. Is coin slot located 48 inches or less from the floor?   ____   ____

                                                      YES   NO

5. Are there telephones equipped for persons with hearing
   disabilities?
   Are these telephones identified as such?   ___   ___
COMMENTS: _____   ___   ___

J. ELEVATORS

                                                      YES   NO

1. If more than a one-story building, are elevators available
   to disabled persons?
   Are they usable by disabled persons?   ___   ___
2. Are all of the controls 48 inches or less from the floor?   ___   ___
3. Are the buttons labeled with raised (or indented) letters   ___   ___
   beside them?
4. Are they easy to push or touch sensitive?   ___   ___
5. Is the cab at least 5 feet by 5 feet?   ___   ___
COMMENTS: _____

K. CONTROLS

                                                      YES   NO

1. Are switches and controls for light, heat, ventilation, windows, draperies, fire alarms, and all similar controls of
   frequent or essential use within the reach of individuals in
   wheelchairs?   ___   ___
COMMENTS: _____

L. IDENTIFICATION

                                                      YES   NO

1. Are raised (or recessed) letters or numbers used to identify
   rooms or offices?   ___   ___
2. Is identification placed on the wall, to the right or left of
   the door?   ___   ___
   Are they at a height between 4 feet 6 inches and 5 feet 6
   inches, measured from the floor?   ___   ___
3. Are doors not intended for normal use, which might prove
   dangerous if a blind person were to exit or enter by them,
   made quickly identifiable to the touch by knurling the
   door handle or knob?   ___   ___
COMMENTS: _____

M. WARNING SIGNALS

                                                      YES   NO

1. Are audible warning signals accompanied by simul-
   taneous visual signals for the benefit of those with hearing
   or sight disabilities?   ___   ___

Compliance Checklist, cont.

COMMENTS: _____

N. HAZARDS

YES   NO

1. When manholes or access panels are open and in use, or
    when an open excavation exists on a site when it is ap-
    propriate to pedestrian traffic, are barricades placed on all
    open sides at least 8 feet from the hazard and warning
    devices installed?   ____   ____

2. Are there no low-hanging door closers that remain within
    the opening of a doorway or that protrude hazardously
    into regular corridors or traffic ways?   ____   ____

3. Are there no low-hanging signs, ceiling lights, fixtures, or
    similar objects that protrude into regular corridors or
    traffic ways?   ____   ____

4. Is lighting on ramps adequate?   ____   ____

5. Are exit signs easily identifiable to all disabled persons? ____   ____

COMMENTS: _____

REFERENCES

*Accessibility—the law and the reality: A survey to test the application and effec-
tiveness of Public Law 90-480 in Iowa.* 1974. Des Moines, IA: Iowa Chapter,
American Institute of Architects. Checklist appears on pp. 63–68.

Eastern Paralyzed Veterans Association. n.d. *Myths and facts about accessibility
for the disabled person.* New York: The Association.

_____. 1984. *Curbcuts: How to design and construct proper curb cuts in Connec-
ticut, New Jersey, New York and Pennsylvania.* New York: The Association.

Eckstein, B. J. *The handicapped funding directory.* Oceanside, NY: Research
Grant Guides, P.O. Box 357, 11572.

Kamisar, H. 1979. *Signs for the handicapped patron.*

Mace, R. L. 1985. *The system: Accessible design and product information system.*
Winston-Salem, NC: Information.

Schroeder, S., and Steinfeld, E. 1979. *The estimated cost of accessible buildings.*
Washington, DC: Department of Housing and Urban Development.

6

Public-Services Programs
for the Disabled

This chapter describes the modifications needed if disabled persons are to use the public services of the library. Some modifications will be facility modifications: lighting, furniture arrangement, sign systems, and service areas. These facility modifications are discussed in Chapter 5. Other modifications will be program activity and service modifications, so that communication aids or material formats accessible to disabled persons are included in those program activities and services.

While many of the public-services suggestions apply to most libraries, we have chosen to stress public-library and school-library media-center public-service applications on the basis of our experiences. Academic librarians will find many of the ideas relevant. Programs and services discussed include library services offered in the library facility, library services for those who cannot come to the library, reference services, special-collection services, and access to information resources located in other libraries and information centers.

PROGRAMS AND SERVICE ACTIVITIES FOR DISABLED PERSONS?

All the programs and services have the *potential* of being useful to disabled persons. As with other groups and individuals, not all programs and services will be used by disabled persons. The important idea is that the *disabled* should make the decision whether to use the library service or participate in the program. That decision should not be made by the library staff (because "none of them would be interested") or because the program or service is held in an inaccessible location or because the activity is presented in a format useless to disabled persons.

This book has presented a systems view of library decision making and how those decisions affect disabled persons, their families, and their advocates. If a library considers decisions about staffing, facilities, materials selection and organization in light of serving disabled persons, many program activities and services will include disabled persons as a normal part of providing services to the public. Throughout this book, we have stressed the centrality of library staff who understand disabling conditions and are sensitive to the needs of persons with those disabilities. Such a library staff will develop activities and services that include disabled persons.

THE IMPACT ON LIBRARY PROGRAMS AND SERVICES

Because of the history of social isolation of disabled persons, it is possible that some individuals will have strong negative feelings about the inclusion of disabled persons in activities and services. It is also true that some disabilities are less "attractive" than others. Some people will be put off by the physical appearance of some disabled persons. As Davis (1961, p. 123) puts it:

> Whether the handicap is overtly and tactlessly responded to as such or, as is more commonly the case, no explicit reference is made to it, the underlying condition of heightened, narrowed awareness causes the interaction to be articulated too exclusively in terms of it. This . . . is usually accompanied by one or more of the familiar signs of discomfort and stickiness: the guarded references, the common everyday words suddenly made taboo, the fixed stare elsewhere, the artificial levity, the compulsive loquaciousness, the awkward solemnity.

Library staff who have been through some of the staff-development activities suggested in Chapter 1 will understand the prejudices and stereotypes of other patrons and will be able to assist them in the process of attitude change. A number of the staff-development activities, films, and kits can be modified for use with patron groups.

When a program involves the same group of persons over time—as in summer reading programs, story hours in branch libraries, or instruction in the context of a school media center—there are a number of techniques for attitude awareness and sensitivity development. Again, Chapter 1 of this book lists a number of attitude-modification activities. As more and more mainstreaming of disabled students has occurred in the schools, educators have developed numerous techniques for preparing other students for disabled children in the classroom or media center.

Many of these difficulties can be overcome by good public relations. Announcements about the program and why disabled persons are being included can be placed on radio stations, TV shows, and news releases. Securing local community leaders' endorsement for such programs can also be effective in reducing anxiety about participation. If the library director and staff have worked closely with the library board in developing program ideas and in the whole systems approach suggested in this book, endorsement by the board should be almost automatic.

In the final analysis, stereotypes and prejudice are overcome through contact with *real* persons who are disabled. If library staff continue to promote isolation through excluding disabled persons from library activities, the stereotypes and prejudice are likely to continue. Taking the risk of offending a few individuals is probably a price worth paying if libraries can contribute to the full participation of disabled persons in our society.

THE FOCUS OF ACTIVITIES AND SERVICES FOR THE DISABLED

Whenever possible, the library staff will want to avoid activities and services that are focused *exclusively* on disabled persons. In public-library services, a number of such focused activities and services were funded through state library agencies, utilizing the Library Services and Construction Act guidelines (Neff, 1984). All too often such "special" or "categorical" funding was granted for a limited time with the expectation that the service would be continued through regular local or state per capita funding for public-library services. If an activity or service is funded as a separate operation using special funding, the activity or service may come to an end when the grant or federal funds are cut or the local economy demands cutbacks in public-agency funding.

In the school-library media setting of public education, efforts should be made to include disabled children in the regular process of library media-center programming. This inclusion will sometimes be difficult because some disabled children will be "tracked" into special classrooms or will have educational and rehabilitation schedules that remove them from the local school setting on a regular basis. For all school librarians, Dresang's "There Are No *Other* Children" (1977) remains the best single summary for inclusion of *all* children in the school-library media program. Lucas and Karrenbrock (1983) also provide many practical suggestions on materials, programs, and cooperation with teachers.

Activities in the school-library media center can be analyzed to see if disabled children *can* be included in the activity as it is now structured. Dequin (1983) offers many suggestions concerning specific media-center activities that can be used to include disabled children and youth in the program of the school-library media center. Several examples of analysis of current school-library media-center activities (based on the authors' experience) follow:

Class Coming to the Library for Books

If there are visually or physically disabled children in the class, are there talking books (from the National Library Service) or other recorded materials, so they can check out materials? Does the library collection contain materials (informational and fictional) that are at appropriate reading levels for all the children? High-interest–low-vocabulary materials can be found, so that everyone can be included. Even children who do not read at all can be provided access to filmstrips, cassette recordings, realia, and models that they can use.

An interesting example of integrated media materials for a variety of children is found in *Kids Kits* (Kids Interest Discovery Studies Kits). This National Diffusion Network Exemplary Program was originated in the Jefferson County School District (Colorado) by JoAnn Peterson (Warder Elementary School, 7840 Carr Drive, Arvala, CO 80005; telephone 303-423-1227). Sets of multimedia materials organized around a theme are designed to elicit active student involvement and independent learning. Because these kits contain a variety of materials and are locally produced, children with a variety of disabilities can use the reading, tactile, model, and realia materials in ways best suited to their interests. Because the materials are collected in boxes (usually banker's boxes), they can be transported to accessible school and home locations.

Storytelling, Book-talking, Puppet-Theatre Programs

If classes come to the library media center for these activities, are the activities presented in ways that are meaningful to visually impaired and hearing-impaired children? Where stories of theatre include objects or characters in special dress, models of these items can be made and passed around the class, so that visually impaired students can touch and view them up close. Paper-doll types of characters with different textured clothing and animal cutouts with fake-fur covering are often used. If there are hearing-impaired children in the class, the school often provides interpreter services or a teacher who can use American Sign Language or Signing Exact English. Cooperative efforts with these people can create storytimes, book-talks, and theatre that will include the hearing-impaired children. Resources are available for the presentation of disabilities and disabled persons in a realistic fashion:

The *Kids on the Block* puppets (1712 EYE Street, NW, Suite 1008, Washington, DC 20006) have received international attention for their use in satisfying children's curiosity about disabilities through open discussions with the puppets. Film and videotapes of Barbara Aiello with the "kids" are available. A new series of children's books by Aiello (based on *Kids on the Block*) is being published by Twenty-First Century Books. The series realistically presents a variety of disabling conditions with children and young people as the main characters.

Pediatric Projects Inc. (P.O. Box 1880, Santa Monica, CA 90406) sells Special Friends—furry stuffed animals, including a monkey in a wheelchair, an elephant with two hearing aids, a koala bear with glasses. TASK (Team of Advocates for Special Kids, 1800 E. La Veta Ave., Orange, CA 92666) sells a guide that includes a script and instructions for making two life-size dolls. PACER (Parent Advocacy Coalition for Educational Rights Center, 4826 Chicago Ave., S., Minneapolis, MN 55417-1055) sells a set of six hand-and-rod-style puppets about 40 inches tall.

Even with excellent selection of materials, it is important to think through ways to integrate children's programs in the library setting. Inclusion of children with disabilities is far more helpful than activities *about* children with disabilities. Some teachers have found that mainstreaming disabled children into the classroom is easier after some preparatory work with the nondisabled children, utilizing puppets, film, and class or small-group discussion.

An increasing number of school television as well as Public Broadcasting Corporation programs come with "closed captioning" and the rights to record and replay these programs in the educational setting. Remember that the copyright provisions vary greatly for programs on television. Commercial network programs and cable programs (including HBO, Cinemax, etc.) are often closed-captioned. The notice "Closed captioned for the hearing impaired" does not imply any recording and playback rights for individuals or schools. When in doubt, the school-library media specialist should check local school-system copyright policies and procedures.

Library Media Center with Learning Centers, Dioramas, or Other Displays

When "centers" for learning are created in the library, they usually involve a set of materials, visuals, and instructions, often including a deck of cards or set of instructions. Visually impaired children can be included in these activities if the instructions are recorded so that they can play back the instruction set. Games need to be rethought, so that the visually impaired child can *feel* the results of dice throws and so on. Raised-dot dice can be purchased; microcomputers can be programmed to produce and verbally announce a number; numbers can be recorded on a cassette recorder and the students told to hold down the play button for a count of 1, 2, 3 and *not* to use the rewind key.

If learning centers and displays take into account the large-print needs of many children (see Chapter 3), the centers will be accessible to many visually impaired children. Location of displays and the height of displays will also influence whether physically handicapped children have access to the center or display. Locate displays where children in wheelchairs can get to them. Test the center by sitting in a 28-inch-high chair and seeing if all the parts of the center can easily be reached. Review the diagrams in Chapter 5 for the reach limitations of children (or adults) in wheelchairs.

Library Media Center Skills Instruction

When basic library-media skills instruction begins, it is typical for students to be introduced to the physical location of various resources in the library media center. Is a raised-line drawing of the physical arrangement of the library media center available for visually impaired children? Are the various sections of the library marked with *reachable* signs that have either raised letters or Braille markings? Is the basic furniture arrangement of the library stable? Remember that visually impaired children use their mobility training to remember where objects are placed. When furniture must be rearranged, visually impaired children should be allowed time to explore the new arrangements.

If the uses of certain media-center resources are being taught as a part of a classroom assignment—how to find and use a dictionary, a thesaurus, the catalog—does the center have large-print editions, recorded editions, or Braille editions for visually impaired students? Are the variety of reading abilities of students represented in the dictionaries, thesauri, and catalog of the center? Consultation with teachers will allow the library-media specialist to arrange for the availability of appropriate formats of materials in the center. Such arrangements often take considerable lead time, so allow time to find, order, and process these materials *prior* to specific instructional times.

School-library media specialists and children's librarians will want to study Eldridge's *R Is for Reading* (1985) for examples of appropriate activities and materials for disabled children. This book results from interviews with disabled children, their parents, special-education teachers, child counselors, reading specialists, and librarians. Many disabled children are part of a rehabilitation-education system that is not focused on getting children and information materials together in the same way that other children are trained to use and enjoy libraries, books, and programs. There are numerous suggestions about what can be done to include these children in library programs and services.

As Brown (1984) has suggested, program activities and services that include disabled persons and provide a needed activity or service to a broader population are much more likely to be sustained in hard times. Such "integration" or "mainstreaming" of activities and services for disabled persons also reduces the tendency for staff and public to think of disabled persons in stereotypical ways.

Rather than develop new services and activities for disabled persons, the library staff should evaluate current services and activities to see how disabled persons can be included in those now being funded. Since programs and services are dependent on the materials collection of the library, previous chapters of this book have discussed the selection and organization of library materials *as if* disabled persons were included in the library's service population.

GUIDELINES FOR INCLUDING DISABLED PERSONS IN LIBRARY PROGRAMS AND SERVICES

Include the Disabled in Groups that Plan and Implement Library Programs

The basic guideline for including disabled persons in library activities and services is to include disabled persons in planning groups that determine the types of activities and services the library offers. Individuals who are involved in the planning and implementation of library services become, almost automatically, advocates for those services in their own communities and groups. Such advocacy is extremely important if the library is to be effective with disabled persons. Because of the ways that society has previously dealt with disabled persons (discussed in Chapter 1), many disabled persons do not regularly use the services of public agencies and are often suspicious of programs and offerings of those agencies. Groups of disabled persons have also developed communication channels *within* their groups that are much more effective than those readily available to the library.

If the planning process has included disabled persons or their advocates as part of the planning team, many potential services will have been evaluated and discarded because (1) the potential service is already available from some other agency or group, (2) the service suggested will not be understood or wanted by disabled persons, and (3) converting the particular service to a format or location usable by disabled persons is excessively expensive. Many great ideas do not survive this evaluation process. It is important that participating library staff *not* become discouraged by this early-planning evaluation process. The process is designed to assist the library staff in avoiding costly mistakes at a later date. Far better that a library staff evaluate and decide not to develop a particular program, than to fund the program, run it for a year, and discover that the community needs thought to exist are not there.

In the planning process for new activities and services, the library staff should carefully evaluate each proprosal for its inclusiveness of diverse groups. While library staff will want to meet the needs of specific individuals and groups, it is important that activities and services be designed to include as much of the service population of the library as possible. Holding a lecture or film series in a meeting room that is inaccessible to disabled persons automatically denies those individuals access. An exhibit that contains no materials that can be touched or smelled automatically excludes the visually impaired and blind individual. Puppet theatre, storytelling, and book-talking can be activities in which children from various language groups can participate, or they can be only in English (no sign language, no Spanish) and automatically exclude those children.

Know the Library Community

Professional literature often contains stories about specific library programs and "new" services offered by a library in another location. Sometimes these services or programs seem like very good candidates for implementation in the local library community. What works in one community may or may not work in another. Prior to any commitment to new program activities, the library director and staff should have an in-depth understanding of the community. There is no reason for starting a program activity if a potentially interested patron group does not exist.

During the past decade, a number of libraries have developed specific services for persons who are disabled in specific ways. One of the authors has been asked to assist libraries in developing services to hearing-impaired or deaf persons. Questions like How many hearing-impaired or deaf persons are in your community? or How many deaf persons in your community use American Sign Language? were often met with the response We do not know. Currently, a number of communities have experienced the immigration of people for whom English is not the native language. Effective programs have been mounted in public libraries and school-library media centers to assist these individuals in acquiring English as an effective second language and to provide reading and instructional materials in their own languages. Libraries should not automatically begin to develop programs for linguistically different groups if such groups do not exist in the community. If there is a different language population, the library staff may be justified in seeking a staff member who has those language skills or training someone on the staff in the language of the potential patrons. Some public libraries in areas where there is a large deaf population have trained staff members in American Sign Language.

To determine if program activities and services *can* include disabled persons, the library staff must have some estimate of the numbers of disabled persons in the community and where they live. Chapter 5 points out that an accessible facility is often unused because disabled persons cannot get to that facility because of limited transportation or inaccessible public-transportation equipment and facilities. Even if there are a large number of disabled persons in the library service area, and even if they are interested in a particular library program, they may not be able to participate because they cannot get to the program.

Library staff will find that other community agencies can help in determining the number of disabled persons in the community. While rules of confidentiality (and sometimes legal requirements) prevent disclosure of specific individual information, many agencies have population statistics on their service population that can assist the library in planning. In the public-library setting, local agencies include

- Health Department
  - Office for Vital Statistics
  - Laboratory Services (immunizations, X-ray, tuberculosis screening)
  - Health Education Services
  - Speech Therapy Departments
  - Office of Occupational Therapy
  - Sexually Transmitted Diseases Clinic
  - Nutrition Services
  - Hearing and Speech Clinic
  - School Health Services
  - Mental Health Clinics
- Social Service Departments
  - Adult Group Care Centers
  - Aged and Disabled Services
  - Aid for the Blind
  - Senior Citizens Offices
  - Veterans' Services
- Office of Community Development and Planning

In the public-school setting, each school system will have an administrative office responsible for maintaining the records of all children legally designated as handicapped. Those files should include an Individualized Education Plan (IEP) for each child, updated annually. Children being considered for school placement as handicapped will be given testing, screening, and review by a system-wide and a school-level committee. School-library media specialists should tap these resources groups for assistance in planning for disabled children in the program of the school-library media center.

Although the particular name of the city or county agency may vary from the list above, offices offering services in these areas will usually be found. Often there is a coordinating council of community-services (or human-services) agencies in an area. These councils will include members from the many private, nongovernmental service agencies and foundations of the area. Membership in this type of council can be an important way for the public-library staff to develop community-analysis strategies.

In the public-school setting, information on the specific community of the local school will be found in the school and its community. In most schools, information on the number and types of disabled children will be available at the school. Because of the enforcement of the Individual Educational Plan process in public education (under Public Law 94-142), all designated disabled or handicapped children should have on file a specific education plan tailored to meet the child's individual educational and developmental needs. The school-library media specialist will need to work closely with the resource-room teacher and with teachers who are working with disabled or handicapped children in mainstreamed settings to discover the specific needs of these children. As more and more children are mainstreamed into regular classroom settings, a variety of media formats will be needed. Many media centers already have a variety of media formats and production possibilities that can be used by disabled and handicapped children without modification (Davie, 1980).

Evaluate All Program Activities and Services

Library programs cost money. The Public Library Association has developed a manual for cost finding in public libraries (Rosenberg, 1985) that will prove helpful to any library trying to determine the actual costs of various activities. Library staff need to know how many people are being served by an activity and what that activity is costing in percentage of overall budget. This evaluation guideline is *not* meant to suggest that the library is to offer only the least expensive services (per patron served), but library directors and professional staff do need to know what programs cost.

Program evaluation on a cost basis informs the library staff about the efficiency of the particular activity. Patron evaluation of the activity will inform the staff about the effectiveness of the activity. Both types of evaluation are essential if the library staff is to continue to meet the needs of its patrons. An expensive program that receives high evaluation ratings from the patrons who participate is a program that may be marketed to other patrons. An inexpensive program that receives low evaluation ratings should not be continued in its present form, no matter how cheap. Program evaluation is not without expense. It involves staff time in cost analysis over a period of time and analysis of patron responses. Without such staff investment, the library director and staff have no means of determining what program activities and services should be emphasized in the future.

REACHING OUT TO DISABLED PERSONS

Ask them! Any library agency planning to offer services to disabled persons needs to devise ways for members of the community who are disabled to comment on such services. If disabled persons have been involved in community analysis and planning of potential services, much information will have been gained about the communication channels of the disabled in the community. The library staff will need to develop public-relations strategies to reach disabled persons with information about programs. Some public-relations strategies follow:

Promoting the Program on Early-Morning Local TV Talk Shows

Most larger communities have an early-morning local news, weather, and human-interest program hosted by well-known local TV personalities. Almost all of these shows welcome the opportunity to promote community, school, and other activities. Careful planning of what particular aspects of the program to promote and sufficient lead time to get on the program are essential.

Creating Local News Stories through News Releases

All libraries receive news releases from a variety of agencies and groups (including the American Library Association). A brief to-the-point news release about a new service or program will often be picked up by the local newspaper. A telephone call to the local newspaper about an upcoming event, followed with a copy of the news release, may result in having the opening of the service covered by a reporter. Illustrated news releases concerning a service being used by one of the trustees or library staff who happens to be disabled are especially effective.

Utilizing Special Communications Channels

Most of the organizations listed in Appendix A will have local groups or chapters that publish newsletters. Many groups of disabled persons have newsletters and other communication services dedicated to their group's interests. For example, parents of disabled children often have a local newsletter distributed to all parents who belong to their advocacy group. Local groups sometimes create radio reading programs for the blind and visually impaired that provide local news, readings of current best sellers, and talk shows by means of an FM subcarrier on local TV channels. The programs are available only to those who have a special receiver (Corporation for Public Broadcasting). As of the end of 1986, there were 155 radio reading services; they formed the Association of Radio Reading Services (1133 20th St., NW, Washington, DC 20036) (Cylke, 1987). The association serves as an information center for radio reading services on staffing, fundraising, programming, outreach and technical aspects of radio reading services.

The National Library Service for the Blind and Physically Handicapped publishes a *Directory of Local Reading Services for the Blind and Physically Handicapped.* The American Foundation for the Blind offers a *Directory of Radio Reading Services* (15 West 16th Street, New York, NY 10011).

Most of these local communication systems welcome news of interest to their constituencies. If the library has *not* involved disabled persons in the planning of the service, the use of these communication channels can be dangerous. Editors and broadcasters on these channels are critical of uninformed or misguided attempts to serve disabled persons.

Creating "Special Events"

Hagemeyer (1975) created a "Deaf Awareness Week" and later "Deaf Heritage Week" at the Washington, DC Public Library, which consisted of special displays related to communication systems for deaf persons and other demonstrations and exhibits. The program was informative for the hearing community about disabilities related to deafness and also served to inform the deaf community about current (and planned) library services available to deaf and hearing-impaired individuals. Friends of Libraries for Deaf Action (FOLDA) continues this library-oriented work with the deaf community. Of special interest to librarians will be *Crossroads* (FOLDA, P.O. Box 50045, Washington, DC 20004-0045), the semiannual newsletter of the organization, and *Communicating with Hearing People* (the "Red Notebook"), which contains materials about the deaf community and how libraries are serving (and can serve) them.

In a similar way, special events at the library—storytelling festivals, musical events, topical discussions, film showings—can be used to publicize new services available to disabled persons. Having a storytime with an interpreter for the deaf or a public showing of a film with captions (remember the restrictions on captioned films from the Captioned Film Service) spreads the word about the new service.

SERVING DISABLED PERSONS WHO CANNOT COME TO THE LIBRARY

In the best of all possible worlds, the answer would be—Take the service to them! However, the costs of individualized home-delivery service need to be carefully analyzed prior to such a commitment. Individual home-delivery services require specialized record keeping, delivery and pickup of items, and staff-time commitments. Delivery of services to home-bound persons may be excessively expensive for many libraries. Many public libraries have utilized LSCA funds to help fund the administration of "homebound" or "shut-in" services. Libraries offering such services typically use volunteers as a major part of the operation.

As a part of the program to serve disadvantaged adults, Schmidt (1974) developed an excellent guide for the planning of volunteer programs to expand library services, the development of volunteer job descriptions, and the training and on-the-job supervision of volunteers. Kuras (1975) presented similar information from a program at the Inglewood Public Library (California). Redmond and Peaco (1981) compiled a checklist of library-service volunteer activities, including collection maintenance, circulation activities, direct services to patrons, outreach services, and administrative duties. They provide an extensive list of materials on volunteer recruitment, training, management, recognition, and placement. Although primarily oriented toward serving visually and physically disabled persons, this publication can be helpful in any situation where a professional staff is considering a volunteer program. Volunteer programs can be *very* specific. For example, Bliss (1986) reports on a program in the Dane County Public Library (Wisconsin) that trains tutors to deal effectively with dyslexic library users. Roy (1984) has summarized the various issues and viewpoints about the use (and abuse) of volunteers in public libraries.

Library professional staffs need to enter the area of volunteer utilization with care. Programs run by volunteers can be a significant part of the library program, especially in these days of limited budgets and more limited staffing. One question that needs to be resolved by the professional staff and the board is If this program is worth running, why can't we get it going with a paid staff? A danger of any volunteer program is that people who fund agencies may think, "Well, they have an excellent volunteer corps. We don't need to fund that program."

There are principles involved in any use of volunteers:

1. Plan the program or service using volunteers very carefully. Library professional staffs need to get the "bugs" out of a program *prior* to utilizing volunteers. There may still be some problems after the volunteers start, but major ones should be thought out ahead of time.

2. Once a program is planned, a guidebook or procedures manual should be developed for volunteers. This manual can serve as one means of training the volunteers for the program. The manual should clearly state (a) the purposes of the program, (b) how to deal with certain situations or problems, (c) questions typically asked, (d) the importance of the volunteer to the success of the program. If the library has clearly defined policies, these might be included as appendixes to the manual.

3. Screen your volunteers carefully. People volunteer for programs for a wide variety of reasons, many of which are good reasons for volunteering; yet it is possible that some individuals seeking to "help" the library and its patrons may need help themselves. While such situations need to be handled with great care, a screening program will allow the professional staff to suggest alternatives to those who are not able to help others.

4. Recruit and train volunteers with the same care that is given to the recruitment and training of staff. When the volunteer works in the library serving the public or visits the homebound, she is "the librarian." Chapter 1 deals with staff development for libraries wishing to include disabled persons in patron groups and staff. It is important that the recruitment and training of volunteers include sessions dealing with the stereotypes and attitudes toward disabled persons. If the volunteers are going to deal with homebound individuals, they will also need training in attitudes toward older persons and death and dying.

5. Give the volunteers an opportunity to change jobs from time to time. Some volunteers will want to stick with what they are doing; others will welcome an opportunity to do some other type of job for a while. With homebound services, the loss of a patron (through death or institutionalization) may signal that the volunteer needs a change of pace.

6. Be sure the volunteers have on-the-job support and supervision. Some volunteer programs in nonprofit agencies use an experienced volunteer to work with new volunteers during their training sessions. No volunteer should feel that the library has dumped a program in his lap and left him to sink or swim on his own. Volunteers need to know that they can get professional staff assistance if they need it.

7. Make sure that there are a variety of recognitions for the volunteers in the program. These can take many forms: service pins, special recognition banquets, news releases, and so on. How volunteers are to be recognized and rewarded and who is responsible for that part of the program should be a part of the planning process. If the library cannot pay for a service, it must develop meaningful rewards for those who provide the service.

8. Be sure that disabled persons have an opportunity to know about and volunteer for library-volunteer activities. The inclusion of disabled persons as part of the volunteer group is in agreement with the philosophy of inclusion stressed throughout this book.

Some state library agencies and local public libraries have utilized a books-by-mail service to reach disabled persons. Reed and Schmidt (1974) developed a guide for books-by-mail services as a part of the Appalachian Adult Education Center program for disadvantaged adults. They suggested that careful cooperative planning be done by library staff, potential clients, and the post office. Extensive publicity was found to be a necessity. In 1974, the cost per book circulated ranged from $.45 to $3.60. Kim and Sexton (1974), reporting a Council on Library Resources conference on books-by-mail held in 1973, noted two distinct types of service: (1) urban or metropolitan services for the homebound, elderly, or institutionalized; and (2) rural programs that reach previously unserved populations. Books-by-mail patrons were found to have the same reading interests as other persons in the local area. Warshasky (1976) reported on a books-by-mail service in Waterbury, Connecticut, which began with a state library grant, utilizing mailings of catalogs to households, newspaper publicity, and postage-paid request cards in the distributed catalogs. Books were mailed in postage-paid returnable bookbags.

In Nova Scotia, Friese (1976) did a cost-benefit comparison of books-by-mail and bookmobile service, and concluded that bookmobile services had the potential for a far greater variety and quality of services. Stephenson (1984) provided a history of the homebound and handicapped services of the Madison Public Library (Wisconsin) from 1961 to 1984.

Suvak (1984) argued that the tremendous growth of mail-order services for consumer goods (growing twice as fast as regular retailing) demonstrates the potential for libraries to adopt books-by-mail services, which will cost less per circulation than regular walk-in services. He doubted that books-by-mail would have any negative impact on bookmobile circulation or the patron's identification with a particular library.

Books-by-mail can reach patrons not reached by any other library service at relatively low cost. The most likely off-site delivery points for libraries will be places where groups of disabled persons meet. These places can include nursing homes, group day-care facilities, sheltered workshops, Goodwill Industries facilities, senior-citizens centers, parks or recreation municipal programs for specific disability groups. If the library can develop deposit collections in facilities where groups meet or live, it is possible to provide library services at fairly reasonable costs. Some libraries' bookmobile or van services stop at nursing homes and other places where groups gather. It is essential to coordinate planning with the host community or private agency sponsoring the primary activity for which the group gathers. For example, in nursing-home facilities, visits need to be coordinated not to interfere with meals, medication delivery, and programs of the nursing-home staff. The International Federation of Library Association has published *Guidelines for Libraries Serving Hospital Patients and*

Disabled People in the Community (1984), which indicates essential features of serving institution-bound persons and suggests alternative ways of setting up services and promoting them in the community and institution.

Where other groups or agencies are visiting regularly in the homes of individuals, it may be possible to coordinate the delivery of library materials with the delivery of other services. Volunteers working with Meals on Wheels have cooperated with library agencies in seeing that requested materials are delivered to individuals and returned to the library. In some communities, home-nursing-care personnel have been cooperative in seeking out library materials for homebound individuals and seeing that the materials are delivered. Homebound services have also been supported by senior-citizen and youth-volunteer groups working directly for the library in an individualized homebound library-materials delivery service.

REFERENCE AND INFORMATION SERVICES
FOR DISABLED PERSONS

Many of the reference services requested by disabled people will be *identical* to those of other patrons. Disabled persons have access to the mass media and will have the same political, social, hobby, and economic interests as other persons. One problem faced by the library reference staff is having the right information, but in a format the disabled cannot use. For example, the appropriate information is often printed in a national or regional newspaper in 6- to 8-point type. This type size means that many visually disabled persons cannot use the information. One solution to this problem is a tabletop copier with enlargement features, so that the article can be copied in a larger size. With some care, newspaper and reference articles can be copied in up to 18–20-point type.

Another format problem will be the *weight* of many reference books. Unfortunately, the reference publisher often saves some costs by cramming a lot of information into a few reference books. Many directories, bibliographies, and indexes will be available only in heavy volumes. This weight factor means that many disabled persons will be unable to handle the reference tool on their own. Again, the copy machine can be helpful in getting the information into a format light enough for disabled persons. As more and more reference tools become available on CD/ROM format or in on-line forms, it is possible for the reference staff to assist the patron in finding and displaying the appropriate information on a screen. Since the microcomputer display goes to a video monitor, the color, intensity, and size of the display can be modified. If the library staff is considering public access to microcomputer-displayed reference information, they will want to consider display screens larger than 13 inches and may also want to consider fairly new overhead projection display devices such as

- Telex Corporation, *Magnabyte* system; models for both IBM and Apple.
- Dukane Corporation, *Magniview 2000;* model will work with both IBM and Apple.
- Sharp Corporation, *QA-25 Computer Projection Panel;* model works with IBM, adapter for Apple.

These projection units (and similar ones) cost between $600 and $1,000, and allow for a very large projection on a screen or wall of anything that appears on the monitor screen. With a Y connector, the monitor can also show what is being projected.

Some visually disabled individuals will not be able to use print in any format and will require materials in recorded or Braille formats. Since many visually disabled persons have experience with recorded formats for personal notetaking, calendars, and outlines, the library staff may want to experiment with volunteer recording services for such patrons. Not everyone can read aloud effectively, but if *information* is the critical point, visually disabled persons will accept a wide range of recording quality. As Chapter 3 points out, a number of Braille and recorded reference tools are available. Many government forms and documents are also available in a recorded or Braille format. If the patron community of the reference department includes enough visually disabled persons who cannot use print in any format, some of these reference tools should be required.

There are expensive computer-based machines that will translate a number of print fonts into sound in a number of languages. The best-known is the Kurzweil (see vendor list in Appendix C), which is now available at about $19,000. Recently a less expensive model with a hand-held camera for scanning several lines of a printer page was introduced. This model is easy to use while sitting with a book at a table. Where there is sufficient demand for reference works in print format, this machine will produce understandable voice output that can also be recorded for later use. The great advantage is that visually handicapped persons can use the *same* reference tools that other people use when they want to use them. The disadvantages include original price and the fact that the machine must be used in an area where mechanical voice output is not a problem for other patrons and staff.

While some of the reference interests of disabled persons are identical to those of other patrons, other concerns and interests are specific to the daily needs of disabled persons, their families, and their friends.

Information on Accessibility of Public Facilities

There are a number of access directors for major cities and areas. Illustrative reference works:

- American Foundation for the Blind (in cooperation with The Museum of American Folk Art). 1989. *Access to art: A museum directory for blind visually impaired people.* Edited by I. Shore. New York: American Foundation for the Blind.
- Cowles, G. 1985. *Accessible wilderness.* Helena, MT: Falcon Press.
- Hecker, H. 1985. *Travel for the disabled: A handbook of travel resources and 500 worldwide access guides.* Portland, OR: Twin Peaks Press.
- Kenney, A. P. 1980. *Access to the past: Museum programs and handicapped visitors.* Nashville, TN: AASLH.
- Weiss, L. 1986. *Access to the world: A travel guide for the handicapped.* rev. ed. New York: Holt.
- _____. 1989 *Washington, D.C. Access.* rev. ed. (Access Travel Guidebooks Series). New York: Access Press.

Information on Legal Matters

Such information is often critically important to parents as they deal with their developing children. Directories of special medical facilities, schools, and assessment centers will be especially helpful. Since not everyone is aware of her civil rights, there are a number of advocacy groups that publish helpful information guides and suggestions:

- Academic Therapy Publications. *Directory of educational facilities for the learning disabled.* Novato, CA: Academic Therapy Publications.
- Amary, I. B. 1980. *Rights of mentally retarded, developmentally disabled to treatment and education.* Springfield, IL: C. C. Thomas.
- Biklen, D. 1970. *Let our children go.* Syracuse, NY: Syracuse University Press.
- Dickman, I. R., and Gordon, S. 1985. *One miracle at a time: How to get help for your disabled child—from the experience of other parents.* New York: Simon & Schuster.
- *Directory of information resources for the handicapped.* 1987. Santa Monica, CA: Ready Reference Press.
- *Directory of living aids for the handicapped.* 1984. Santa Monica, CA: Ready Reference Press.

- Dubow, S. 1987. *Legal rights of hearing-impaired people.* Washington, DC: Gallaudet University Press.
- *Exceptional Parent Magazine.* 605 Commonwealth Ave., Boston, MA 02215.
- Goldberg, S. 1982. *Special education law: A guide for parents, advocates and educators.* New York: Plenum.
- Katz, A. H., and Martin, K. 1982. *A handbook of services for the handicapped.* New York: Greenwood Press.
- Markel, G. P., and Greenbaum, J. 1979. *Parents are to be seen and heard: Assertiveness in educational planning for handicapped children.* San Luis Obisbo, CA: Impact.
- National Center for the Law and the Deaf. 1984. *The legal rights of hearing impaired people.* Washington, DC: Gallaudet University Press.
- Porter Sargent Group. 1986. *Directory for exceptional children.* 11th ed. Boston: Porter Sargent.
- Rothstein, L. F. 1984. *Rights of physically disabled persons.* Colorado Springs, CO: Shepherd-McGraw.
- Russell, L. M. 1983. *Alternatives: A family guide to legal and financial planning for the disabled.* Evanston, IL: First Publications.

Information Concerning Specific Conditions

When families are first confronted with a diagnosis of a disabling condition, they may want more information about that condition, other individuals who have that condition, and so on. This is particularly true of adults as they face disabling conditions related to aging. The reference staff will want to evaluate their reference collection in the area of consumer health information, medical dictionaries, and other health-related tools. Some of the most up-to-date information will be found in the publications of national agencies dedicated to services for specific disability groups. A list of some of these groups will be found in Appendix A. The publications lists of these groups should be regularly reviewed by the reference staff.

Some illustrative reference tools:

- Ayrault, E. W. 1977. *Growing up handicapped: A guide for parents and professionals to helping the handicapped child.* New York: Seabury Press.
- Children with handicaps, parent and family issues. *News Digest* (November 1985). National Information Center for Handicapped Children and Youth. Box 1492, Washington, DC 20013.
- Cunningham, C., and Sloper, P. 1981. *Helping your exceptional*

baby: A practical and honest approach to training a mentally handicapped baby. New York: Pantheon.
- Hale, G., ed. 1979. *Source book for the disabled: An illustrated guide to easier more independent living for physically disabled people, their families and friends.* London: Imprint Books (Paddington Press in the U.S.).
- Kastein, S., Spaulding, I., and Scharf, B. 1980. *Raising the young blind child: A guide for parents and educators.* New York: Human Science Press.
- Murphy, A. T. 1981. *Special children, special parents: Personal issues with handicapped children.* Englewood Cliffs, NJ: Prentice- Hall.
- Mykleburst, H. L. 1979. *Your deaf child: A guide for parents* (American Lecture Series). Springfield, IL: Thomas.
- Sargent, J. V. 1981. *An easier way: Handbook for the elderly and handicapped.* Ames, IA: Iowa State University Press.
- Segel, M. 1987. *In time & with love: A guide for parents of preterm and handicapped children.* New York: New Market Press.
- Thompson, C. T. 1987. *Raising a handicapped child: A helpful guide for parents of the physically disabled.* New York: Ballantine.

Families are often concerned about appropriate and useful clothing for their disabled child. The following catalogs offer a number of options:

- Exceptionally Yours
  22 Prescott St.
  Newtonville, MA 02160
- Special Clothes
  P.O. Box 4220
  Alexandria, VA 22303
- Techni-Flair
  P.O. Box 40
  Cotter, AK 72626
- Sitting Pretty, Sitting Proud
  3637 Arundel Circle
  Ventura, CA 93003

Other resources in the area of clothing:

- Information Center for Individuals with Disabilities. *Clothing and accessories for people with special needs.* Boston: The Center, 20 Park Plaza, Room 330, Boston, MA 02116.

- National Easter Seal Society. *Self-help clothing for children who have physical disabilities.* Chicago: The Society, 2023 W. Ogden Ave., Chicago, IL 60612.
- President's Committee on the Employment of Persons with Disabilities. *Clothing for handicapped people: An annotated bibliography and resource list.* Washington, DC: The Committee. (Available from the Division of Clothing, Textiles and Interior Design, University of Arizona, Tuscon, AZ 85721)

PROVIDING ACCESS TO LOCAL HISTORY OR GENEALOGICAL COLLECTIONS

Many library agencies have developed an extensive collection of materials related to local history and family life. Some of these agencies are also repositories for the archives of local groups and corporations. The physical nature of historic materials and the ways archival materials are stored create some unique problems for disabled persons.

First, some materials are extremely fragile in their original state. Whenever possible, these materials should be copied for use by patrons or made into some type of microform that can be used with a microform reader. If a microfilm reader has good optical quality, disabled persons will be able to read what is on the screen. When library staff are considering the purchase of microfilm readers, they should evaluate not only the optical quality (the quality of the image projected) but also the location of controls on the machine. Can a person in a wheelchair read all the controls? Can that person load the film into the machine? If the machine is a reader/printer, can he reach the coin slot? Many local-government records and genealogical materials are now available in microform editions, and this format should be considered not only for convenience of storage but also for ease of access for disabled persons.

Second, archival records come in a bewildering array of sizes and shapes. Usually these records are placed in folders and then in archival boxes. This form of acid-free storage protects the materials but also makes their use very difficult for many disabled or elderly persons. Where a library has extensive archival materials available, individual assistance will often be needed to extract the appropriate materials from the box, then the folder. Some institutions are exploring the possibility of CD/ROM or larger videodisc storage for archival records and large statistical tables. As this trend develops, access to such materials will depend not on physical storage but upon the quality of the video monitor and the microcomputer software available to search for the appropriate items.

Some disabled people will not be able to use special-collection materials in their current formats, because of visual disabilities or physical disabilities that prevent the use of print materials. Very little local-history, archival, or genealogical material is recorded at the regional or local level. Public libraries wanting to make local history or genealogy available to these patrons will have to establish a recording program that places the needed information on an audio cassette. Obviously, libraries cannot respond to every individual request for information by making a recording. Some libraries have volunteer readers who are "on call" to read information to library patrons. More typically, library reference staff note frequently requested materials and arrange to have volunteer readers make recordings of those materials, so that a number of patrons can use them. Some visually impaired individuals will be able to use these materials if they can be enlarged with a copy machine. Again, it is most likely that enlarged copies will be made (and filed) for those items most often requested.

INTERLIBRARY LOANS AND NETWORK SERVICES

More and more library agencies are participating in library networks that allow relatively easy access to materials found in other libraries. Libraries are also using on-line access to reference indexes and full-text materials as well as various telecommunication systems to share information. If disabled persons are not to be left out of this increased access to information, some thought needs to be given to providing information services to disabled persons on an area or regional basis.

Many libraries have policies that *exclude* recorded or visual materials from interlibrary-loan agreements. These may arise from a legitimate concern about loss of valuable information resources; however, these policies need careful consideration since visually and physically disabled persons may not be able to use the materials if the policy is enforced. If libraries produce special materials (recordings, raised-line maps, Braille materials, etc.) for their disabled patrons, they need to develop union lists of these materials, so that all of the libraries in a region or network will be able to access these materials. Often such a union list can cut the labor costs in every library in the network.

As more and more networking is done electronically through machine-readable files, libraries need to focus on how to display information for patrons. Since libraries have a dismal history of displaying microforms in useful ways, care should be taken to develop visual systems that do not cause undue hardship for users of the systems. Display systems can be purchased and located so that there is a minimum of glare and the size of the display can be controlled by the user. This text is written on a display monitor that can be adjusted for size of the letters, colors, background and border. For many individuals, such control means the difference between getting information and being denied that information.

The wide variety of textual, image, and audio information that can be stored and displayed on CD/ROM and videodisc equipment is just beginning to be explored. These devices will allow publishers to publish text in a variety of fonts and sizes together with audio output and illustrations, including icons, actual photographs, digitally enhanced photographs, and television sequences relevant to the text. As these products develop, *multimedia* will take on a new meaning. Librarians can explore some of the implications of this new technology by reading Miller's *The New Optical Media in the Library and the Academy Tomorrow* (1986). Chapter 7 explores some of the implications of the new information technologies for disabled persons.

In the school-library media setting, competence goals often include the ability to identify, find, and use information for classroom assignments, career assessment, and leisure activities. As more and more information becomes available on-line or in CD/ROM format, these competence goals are being expanded to include the use of telecommunication systems as a means of communicating with other students in other places and retrieving relevant information. On-line systems, electronic bulletin boards, and other microcomputer-based telecommunication systems are being recommended because these systems can

- motivate students to participate;
- provide a peer audience for what is written (by transmitting messages to other schools or individuals);
- provide reading experience (you must understand the screen messages to proceed);
- provide reading practice that can improve reading rate;
- develop comprehension and vocabulary skills;
- broaden the number and depth of resources available to the student;
- develop decision-making and critical-thinking skills (sequencing, "what-are-the-parts-of," priority, "what-to-do-if" skills);
- familiarize students with the operation of computer-based systems now commonly used in business, government, and industry.

It is not necessary that instruction begin with actual on-line or telecommunication activities that require a telephone, model, and microcomputer. A number of simulations of bulletin-board and on-line data bases are available. Illustrative of these simulations:

Donnelly's Bulletin Board Simulation. Gerald Donnelly, High Point City Schools, High Point, NC 27261 (919-885-5161).
    Simulates using an electronic bulletin board.

The Electronic Village. EXSYS, 2728 23 St., Greeley, CO 80631 (303-330-8021).
    Simulates electronic bulletin boards.
Kidmail. Wayne Ayers, Culver City High School, 4401 Elenda St., Culver City, CA
    90230 (213-839-4361).
    Simulates electronic mail.
Microsearch. ERIC Clearinghouse, 030 Huntington Hall, Syracuse University,
    Syracuse, NY 13210.
    Simulates on-line searching of ERIC data bases for articles and journal
    references.
The Information Connection. Grolier Electronic Publishing, Sherman Turnpike,
    Danbury, CT 06816 (800-858-8858).
    Simulates online reference using *Academic American Encyclopedia.*

School-library media specialists have developed on-line searching programs for their faculties and students. Aversa (1985) summarizes the
research in this area and makes some recommendations for school-library
media specialists beginning this type of service. She urges library-media
specialists to involve teachers in the planning of curriculum units that require on-line searching, so that on-line instruction can be based on actual
student needs. Tenopir (1986a, 1986b) describes some of the most active
school programs that introduce elementary and secondary students to on-
line searching. Curriculum guides for on-line searching as a part of the
overall curriculum are available; for examples, see Newman and Matomatsee (1985) and Schrader (1985). Successful use of on-line bibliographic
data-base systems will involve

• Assessing carefully the comparative costs of various vendors.
Almost all vendors offer special rates to educational institutions that are
much lower than regular commercial rates.

• Analyzing the indexes and abstracts that are available. It is possible
to use technical financial information and scientific journal abstracts but
much more likely that teachers and students will use magazine and
newspaper indexes, and abstracts of more popular (and available) journals.

• Including teachers in planning curriculum units that require the use
of both print and on-line resources to make reports, compile bibliographies, or study some aspect of current affairs. On-line services should be
presented as another bibliographic reference tool.

• Designing a step-by-step process for student searching that includes
developing a search strategy on paper, having that strategy evaluated, and
then going on-line. This process lets teacher and student evaluate the thinking process and develop writing skills, and holds on-line costs down.

• Making policy decisions about who does the searching—the library-
media specialist, trained student aides, or the teacher and the student.
Remember that each searcher requires training. Whenever financially possible, the students should do the searching, so that they not only develop the

critical thinking skills related to search strategy but also receive the rewards (and punishments) of their efforts directly.

• Publicizing the service and the results of teachers' and students' use of the on-line system in order to create greater demand and funding.

• Developing policies to deal with issues of copyrighted materials, noninstructional use of the system, and related issues.

School-library media specialists will find that involving disabled children and youth in on-line services and related technologies is not difficult. Many disabled students have had experience with keyboards (on computers or calculators) and will bring that experience to on-line searching. Few students type with any degree of accuracy or speed, so that difference between disabled and nondisabled students will not be noticeable. The ability to use the microcomputer to find something useful (and sometimes entertaining) can motivate students as they begin to access on-line systems. Since search strategy (thinking skills) rather than physical skills determines the success of an on-line search, disabled students are placed in a potentially equal situation.

SUMMARY

This chapter has presented an outline of ways disabled persons can be integrated into the ongoing programs and services of libraries. The chapter is only suggestive of some possibilities. If the library trustees, director, and professional staff are committed to integrating disabled persons and have regular contact with persons who are disabled (as staff members and patrons), many other ways of integrating the library into the lives of disabled persons will emerge.

REFERENCES

Aversa, E. 1985. Teaching online searching: A review of recent research and some recommendations for school media specialists. In Current research column, edited by J. C. Mansell, *School Media Quarterly* 13(3–4), 215–220.

Bliss, B. A. Dyslexics as library users. 1986. *Library Trends* 35(2), 293–302.

Brown, D. 1984. Serving disabled people in public libraries. *Public Libraries* 23(10), 8–10.

Corporation for a Public Broadcasting. n.d. *Radio reading services for the print handicapped.* Washington, DC: The Corporation, 1111 Sixteenth Street, Washington, DC 20036. The Corporation for Public Broadcasting also produces a newsletter, *SCALogram.*

Cylke, F. K. 1987. Access to information for blind and physically handicapped persons: Recent developments. In Simora, F., ed., *The Bowker annual of library and book trade information.* New York: Bowker, 93–101.

Davie, J. F. 1980. *A survey of school library media resources for exceptional students in Florida Public Schools.* Doctoral dissertation, Florida State University.

Davis, F. 1961. Deviance disavowal: The management of strained interaction by the visibly handicapped. *Social problems* 9, 123.

Dequin, H. C. 1983. *Librarians serving disabled children and young people.* Littleton, CO: Libraries Unlimited.

Dresang, E. T. 1977. There are no *other* children. *School Library Journal* 24, 19–23.

Eldridge, L. 1985. *R is for reading: Library service to blind and physically handicapped children.* Washington, DC: National Library Service for the Blind and Physically Handicapped.

Friese, D. 1976. *Evaluation of public library bookmobile services in rural areas in comparison to a books-by-mail service.* ERIC Document Reproduction Service no. ED 125 633.

Hagemeyer, A. 1975. *Deaf Awareness Handbook for Public Librarians.* Washington, DC: Public Library of the District of Columbia.

International Federation of Library Associations, 1984. *Guidelines for libraries serving hospital patients and disabled people in the community. IFLA professional reports, No. 2.* The Hague, Netherlands: IFLA. ERIC Document Reproduction Service no. ED 264 864.

Kim, C. H., and Sexton, I. M. 1974. *Books by mail service: A conference report (Las Vegas, Nevada, June 23, 1973).* Washington, DC: Council on Library Resources. ERIC Document Reproduction Service no. ED 114 058.

Kuras, C. 1975. *Volunteer assistance in the library.* Inglewood, CA: Inglewood Public Library. ERIC Document Reproduction Service no. ED 111 399.

Lucas, L., and Karrenbrock, M. H. 1983. *The disabled child in the library: Moving into the mainstream.* Littleton, CO: Libraries Unlimited.

Miller, D. C. 1986. *The new optical media in the library and the academy tomorrow.* Portland, OR: Fred Meyer Charitable Trust, 1515 SW Fifth Ave., Suite 500, Portland, OR 97201.

Neff, E. 1984. *Library services to physically handicapped persons.* Washington, DC: U.S. Department of Education, Center for Libraries and Education Improvement, Division of Library Programs, State and Public Library Services Branch. In-house typescript.

Newman, J., and Matomatsee, N. 1985. *Research goes to school II: How to go online to the information database.* Olympia, WA: State Superintendent of Public Instruction. ERIC Document Reproduction Service no. ED 252 242.

Pennsylvania State Library. 1985. *Pennsylvania online: A curriculum guide for school media centers.* Harrisburg: The State Library. ERIC Document Reproduction Service no. ED 264 887.

Peterson, J. C. 1982. *KIDS KITS: Kids Interest Discovery Study KITS.* Arvada, CO: The Jefferson County School District, Lakewood, CO.

Redmond, L., and Peaco, F., comp. 1981. *Becoming a volunteer: Resources for individuals, libraries and organizations: Reference circular 81-2.* Washington, DC: National Library Service for the Blind and Physically Handicapped.

Reed, M. J., and Schmidt, S. K. 1974. *Books by mail: Moving the library to disadvantaged adults.* Morehead, KY: Appalachian Adult Education Center. ERIC Document Reproduction Service no. ED 098 978.

Rosenberg, P. 1985. *Cost finding for public libraries: A manager's handbook.* Chicago: American Library Association.

Roy, L. 1984. Volunteers in public libraries: Issues and viewpoints. *Public Library Quarterly* 5, 29–40.

Schrader, S. 1985. *A curriculum guide for online database searching with high school students.* Ankeny, IA: Heartland Education Agency. ERIC Document Reproduction Service no. ED 254 373.

Schmidt, S. K. 1974. *Utilizing volunteers in expanding services to disadvantaged adults: Library services guide number 5.* Morehead, KY: Morehead State University, Appalachian Adult Education Center. ERIC Document Reproduction Service no. ED 098 979.

Stephenson, M. 1984. Development of services to the homebound and handicapped at Madison Public Library. *Wisconsin Library Bulletin* 79, 132–133.

Suvak, D. 1984. Fourteen percent growing: The case for mail library service. *Library journal* 109(12), 1294–1297.

Tenopir, C. 1986a. Online searching in schools. *Library Journal* (Feb. 1): 60–61.

―――. 1986b. Student online data base searching, part I. *Computing Teacher* (April): 18–19. See also *Computing Teacher* (May 1986): 39–40, 87.

Warshasky, S. 1976. *Books-by-mail using a mail order book catalog. A project report.* Waterbury, CT: Silas Bronson Library. ERIC Document Reproduction Service no. ED 129 275.

7

Information Services
for the Disabled Person
in the Information Age

Throughout this book, references have been made to a variety of technological devices, usually related to computers, that enable disabled persons to have better access to and use of information resources. The publishers of information materials are in the process of revolutionizing the formats of information. Any librarian visiting national library meetings and going through the exhibits over the past two years has found increasing advertisement for CD/ROM formats to store large, often retrospective data bases previously published in bulky, hard-to-use printed volumes.

Major on-line systems vendors are developing subsets of their data bases to be distributed to CD/ROMs. Developers of mass-data-storage equipment have begun to write about digital tapes (now available in audio-cassette format at the local record store) as the large-data-base storage and retrieval medium of the future. Formerly slow modem communication (approximately 10 characters per second) is now routinely handled at much higher speeds (120 to 960 characters per second). A number of education departments around the country are experimenting with the use of communication satellites for the delivery of interactive classroom instruction. Drawings and writings on a large "white" board can now be copied immediately for handouts in a meeting or transmitted to a similar board in another location. Information is now gathered, stored, retrieved in electronic media.

A bewildering array of electronic media-formats has emerged. This chapter looks at some of the possible developments in the library's access to information and the impact of the various formats on disabled persons' access to information. Predicting the future is a risky business because no one has been there and no one can say how fast developments in information and communication technology will proceed. However, there are some emerging trends and current activities which seem to have long-term implications.

INFORMATION FORMATS AFFECTING LIBRARIES MOST

So many different formats have emerged over the past few years that it is difficult to tell which will have a lasting impact on the library field. The information-publishing world seems to be in a situation similar to the audiorecording industry thirty years ago when recording formats were 78 rpm, 45 rpm, and 33⅓ rpm with different sizes and types of disks.

Some experts in the field see the CD/ROM as "the most significant advance in publishing technology in the last four hundred years" (Gale, 1985, quoting a Phillips executive at an Information Industry Association meeting). It is clear that vast amounts of previously printed information (up to 225,000 pages or more than 730 million bytes of data) can be stored on one CD/ROM disk and that random-access search software can rapidly retrieve specific information from the disk. Most current microcomputers can have a CD/ROM player attached to them so that disks can be searched. H. W. Wilson Company has made its full line of on-line indexes available in CD/ROM format, and most other vendors of on-line services (OCLC, DIALOG, etc.) are making some data bases available in CD/ROM format. Silver Platter Information Services offers a range of data base services, including the ERIC data base; *Psychological Abstracts;* NICEM indexes; the medical-literature data bases of Elsevior Scientific Publishers, Occupational Health and Safety data bases; and *Sociological Abstracts* — all with regular update replacement CD/ROMs. Some of the advantages of this format of information include

- Large storage capacity.
- Lack of wear on the disk; because the player uses a light source, no wear or tear on the disk occurs during playing.
- Ability to encode both text and (real, not synthesized) speech on the same disk; makes true interactive programs possible and could have speech output for the visually impaired a natural part of text output.
- Low cost for large data bases; Library Corporation is publishing MARC data on CD/ROM at about 1/10th of the cost of previous microform publication (Murphy, 1985).

A number of companies are utilizing the larger laser videodisc technology to store over 500,000 pages of data (Carney, 1985). The CD/ROM or larger videodisc offers libraries the opportunity to store and retrieve very large data bases of information typically stored in cumbersome printed volumes. Where this data is stable or retrospective, the laser-disc technology will be utilized extensively in libraries because of the efficient retrieval capabilities and the saving of storage space. Price-Wilkins

(1987), reviewing the OPTEXT system for storing the *Code of Federal Regulations* with quarterly updates, sees this technology effectively replacing the printed format of such large government (and legal) data bases. He states that the CD/ROM format and software replace an awkward and imposing printed source with one source that is both the index and the source itself, offering both keyword and citation access. Similarly, large encyclopedic sources can be made available in this format. Digital optical publishing and its implications for publishers and libraries have been explored by Miller (1987).

　　Previous electronic storage systems have focused on either pictures and other iconographic materials (videotape, film) or digital storage of textual materials (floppy disks, hard-disk storage). The Library of Congress has been experimenting with laserdisc technology in analog form to test the ability of this technology to preserve pictorial information and improve patrons' access to these pictorial resources (Parker, 1985). Over 100,000 images can be stored on a two-sided disk while the user is provided with random access to the file of pictures and can "freeze" a picture on the screen. Cash (1985) reports that museums are also storing pictures of museum pieces on laserdiscs. The Council on Library Resources (1985) has issued a major study of the application of laserdisc technology to library files and operations.

NEW ELECTRONIC FORMATS

In many areas of expensive publication, such as the journals related to basic research where many different information messages are sent to relatively few people, the scientific and professional communities will probably turn to some form of electronic storage of information and distribution by subsidized on-line systems, including electronic bulletin boards or CD/ROM formats. In other areas, librarians will see information published in print format and also available "full-text" through on-line systems. Encyclopedias, newspapers, and some popular magazines are now routinely available in two formats. If consumers will pay for on-line access to full-text versions of periodicals and books, there are publishers who will make these formats available. The hard questions for librarians are (1) how to justify the costs of the electronic format and (2) if the electronic format is available, can the library continue to subscribe to the print format. Some academic reference departments are facing the same problem with basic-reference indexes and abstracts being available on-line (for a fee) and in print ("free") in the same library. Some patrons will pay a fee *not* to use regular reference tools.

　　In the mass market of trade publications and periodicals, other formats will be much slower in taking over the market. There will be budget competition among the various formats. Most librarians operate with a fairly fixed acquisitions budget and are increasingly forced to make difficult choices about what they will select. Some indication of the trends can be seen by watching the circulation of books recorded on audiocassettes or videocassettes. Lettner (1985) surveyed the use of videocassettes in academic and public libraries and found the use of videocassettes (including checking-out of cassettes) increasing. Julien (1985) described the planning and implementation of a videocassette-lending service at the King County Library System (Washington), including packaging, circulation, dealing with overdues, and dealing with damaged tapes. In 1986, Avallone and Fox surveyed public and academic libraries about the use of audio- and videocassettes, and reported an increased use and budget commitment to these formats as well as a number of problems related to theft, damage, competition with local stories, and censorship.

If recorded books become increasingly popular, librarians will need to consider how much of the acquisitions budget should remain in print materials. The same problem has faced public libraries that began the circulation of videotapes and faced the problem of how to allocate funds to different formats. In the long run, the patrons of the library will indicate the formats they prefer *if* they have information about and access to the various formats. For disabled persons, librarians must consider not only the issue of general public demand but also the issue of limited access. Where a format can be easily used by both disabled and nondisabled persons, that format is the format of preference.

In almost all cases, local, state, and regional information resources will continue to be distributed in print format because of their low volume of publication and very limited distribution. Local school-library media centers and public libraries will be responsible for format conversions.

CONVERTING INFORMATION IN ELECTRONIC FORM

Once information is in a machine-readable format, the number of conversions is limited only by the ability of the library to purchase computer-related communication aids that will convert digital data into large images on screens, large (and very large) print on paper, Braille output, and voice output. Obviously, no library will purchase all the available communication peripherals. The basis for decisions about conversions will be based on an assessment of the information-processing disabilities of people who use information in the library.

Essentially, these decisions will result from consultation with the disabled patrons and conversations among the public-services library staff about difficulties encountered in attempting to provide information to patrons. As the librarians become more experienced with their disabled patrons, they will be able to recommend specific computer-related peripherals. It is likely that information will be displayed on some type of a cathode ray tube (CRT). As Miller (1983) has pointed out, there are a number of differences between the typical typewriter workstation and the CRT-display workstation now appearing in many library workrooms and public-service areas:

- CRT units with microcomputers are often larger and require more space for the printer.
- The keyboard of the microcomputer may be located farther away from the screen than the typewriter keyboard is from the typewriter platen. Microcomputer keyboards are often portable (because of a long connecting cable or infrared system).
- Lighting, glare, and contrast are much more noticeable with the CRT screen.

Assuming that many library staff members and patrons will use workstations with CRT screens attached to microcomputers, librarians should think through the design of such workstations to include the following (adapted from Miller, 1983, pp. 154–155).

- Viewing distance from the CRT should be 450–500 mm. This distance may need to be varied for visually impaired users and will in part depend on the size of the text on the screen and various color and black/white/gray contrasts (see Figure 7.1).
- The height of the CRT and its angle vis-à-vis the operator should be adjustable. Physically disabled users may need to have the height adjusted by placing the CRT next to the microcomputer or keyboard. A wide variety of adjustable holders for CRT monitors can be purchased. Often a board or book placed under the back of the CRT will be adjustment enough.
- The keyboard height should allow the user's arms to form at least a 90-degree angle (or more) for ease of use. Since many disabled users will be seated in a wheelchair, the table height may need adjustment to accomplish this angle. Keyboards with long connecting cords can sometimes be placed on work surfaces attached to the arms of the wheelchair to allow comfortable reach of all the keys and a place to rest the forearms.
- Seating for the user should be adjustable to allow the user's legs to form at least a 90-degree angle at the knee. Some disabled users will need to use the keyboard and CRT while standing or with the seat raised as much as 12 inches more than typical.
- Glare is a problem for all CRT users. Librarians should consider

buying CRTs with antiglare screens, screen filters, or screen hoods. Indirect nonfluorescent lighting is helpful.

FIGURE 7.1   CRT Workstation

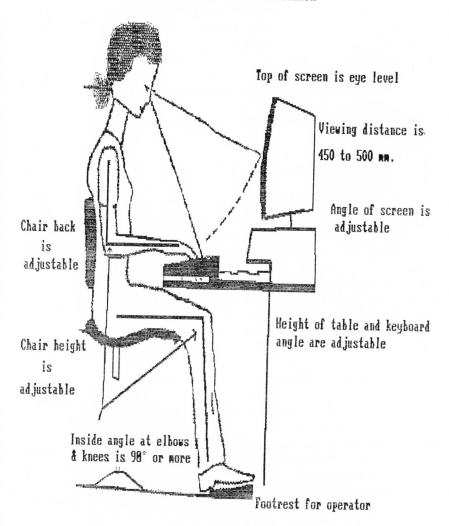

Top of screen is eye level

Viewing distance is 450 to 500 mm.

Angle of screen is adjustable

Chair back is adjustable

Height of table and keyboard angle are adjustable

Chair height is adjustable

Inside angle at elbows & knees is 90° or more

Footrest for operator

Michaels (1987) makes similar suggestions in her review of adjustable furniture (including video-display workstations) in light of the revised draft of *American National Standard for Human Factors Engineering of Visual Display Terminal Workstations.*

Another safe assumption for librarians is that displays of information will need to be enlarged for an increasing number of patrons and staff. As the population grows older, visual problems related to size of print (in books or on screens) become a problem for more and more people. Librarians will find Pifer and Bronte's *Our Aging Society: Paradox and Promise* (1986) a good source of information for thinking about the effects of the population explosion in the over-65 group. Some of these effects:

- What is considered "old" is being redefined. "Old" once meant 55 or 60. It now means 75 and older.
- Women live an average of seven years longer than men and often live alone on their own retirement income for a number of years.
- Health-care concerns have become a critical concern for the very old in our society. The number of persons with health problems and physical disabilities (visual, auditory, and orthopedic) will increase tremendously over the next decades.

The library implications of these changes are that many people face a new period in life and that libraries will have an opportunity to provide information that can help people make appropriate adjustments to that new period. When earlier generations reached 60, the future was retirement and (maybe) leisure activities. Now people reaching that age face 20 to 25 years of active life, often at the end of a career. Libraries prepared with appropriate materials in appropriate formats will be able to help these people plan, fill their lives with new interests, start new careers, or offer services to the community. An ever-increasing number of people will need barrier-free access to library facilities and public-service areas, and will require various kinds of visual aids (large-type, magnification, etc.) to use the library's resources effectively.

Since one of the major problems facing this new generation is visual acuity and related visual problems requiring larger text, librarians will need to explore the methods for enlarging the whole display:

- Larger CRT monitors, so that all text is of a larger size; often a larger screen display combined with pushing the "caps lock" key, so that text is in all upper case, will be sufficient.
- Various types of table-mounted magnifiers with CRT displays to allow viewing by portions of a screen display; some of the illuminated magnifiers will cause problems of glare, so each one must be evaluated in action.
- Software programs that allow for all text sent to the screen to appear in larger letters and allow the user to control the amount of text displayed on the screeen (see the list of vendors in Appendix C).

- Plasma-display units for use with overhead projectors (see Chapter 6) to display computer output on a screen or wall.

Other conversions of electronic data files are possible, but most disabled persons will be well served by one of these conversions.

PERSONS WHO ARE INSTITUTIONALIZED OR HOMEBOUND

Participation is the simplest definition of the potential of the information age for these persons. As more and more information is created, stored, and organized in electronic formats, disabled persons will be able to "read" information from a microcomputer (with a modem) or a terminal in their homes or from a workstation in an institution. Since many of the systems will allow for interaction between computers, the disabled person can participate in computer-based teleconferences, instructional programs offered by schools and universities in an on-line format, and other avocational or recreational systems available on systems such as *Source* or *CompuServe*.

If libraries are to participate in the process of distributing information for educational, vocational, and personal purposes, librarians must become involved in the planning and development of local and regional teleconferencing and home delivery of information. Most local cable companies provide community access to specific cable channels at certain times each week. Some libraries have participated in these community programming efforts. Kenney (1983) summarizes some of these efforts and notes that public libraries seem to be at the forefront of efforts to use cable television effectively. School-library media specialists can participate in home-instruction programs where resources are delivered to the student or the student participates in the class through a telephone connection. Close cooperation with the home-instruction coordinator for the school system will be essential.

Where states or regions are developing "distance education" programs so that all public schools in a region or state can have access to a standard curriculum, the opportunities for library–media-skills training and library programming such as storytelling, book talking, and story theater can be developed by school-library media personnel working with regional or state school personnel who are developing programs for distribution. Ming (1986) and Ming and MacDonald (1987) have reported on distance education of library personnel for public and school libraries in Alberta, Canada. Some examples of program possibilities:

1. Meeting student competence requirements through distance education. Many states have required student competencies in the area of library-

media skills that can legitimately be made part of any public distance-education distribution system. In areas where individual schools do not have full-time library-media specialists, the rationale for such programming is even more justified: How are these students to acquire these skills otherwise?

2. Sharing the results of student use of telecommunication systems including on-line searching. As school-library media centers develop programs involving telecommunication systems and on-line searching, the results of student telecommunication efforts (stories, poems, programs, etc.) can be shared through the distance-education system. When a student develops a bibliography related to an assignment, that bibliography could be shared through the distance-education program.

3. Sharing student activities through television. In some school-library media programs, students are trained in storytelling, dramatic productions, or book talking. The *Reading Rainbow* series on public television has certainly proved that children describing books to other children can create great interest. Having students develop book reports, skits, news programs, story theater, and original writings that can be transmitted over the distance-education system to other schools (and even other states) can be an effective way to promote reading and appreciation of books and literature. When these activities are part of integrated language-arts and media-skills programs, the results benefit the students in several ways. Students often work harder and produce better results when their activities are going to be seen by their peers. Age does not seem to be a critical factor in these activities. One of the authors taught kindergarten and first graders the elements of *LOGO* and then had students "share" their programs with other students. The effect of that "sharing" activity showed in improved *LOGO* displays and improved oral-language skills in explaining the program so that other students could do the program.

4. Distributing video programs of "national" leaders in storytelling, media programming, and so on. Regional distribution of nationally famous storytellers, or media staff development could also be distributed through the system.

THE COST FOR LIBRARIES

The question may be Can libraries afford *not* to get into information-age technologies? If libraries continue to do the same things in the same ways as education, business, and industry move into new ways of finding, storing, and communicating information, libraries will become less and less useful to a larger and larger number of people. Newer information technologies are expensive, and the costs of hardware and software will continue to decline as more and more customers buy into the technology.

Microcomputers provide an interesting example of that trend. In the mid-1970s, a fully equipped microcomputer with disk drives, 64,000 bytes of memory, and a printer cost between $5,000 and $7,000. Even the emerging TRS-80, Model I, Level II machine with 16,000 bytes of memory cost nearly $1,000 without a printer. Recently, an IBM-like microcomputer with 640,000 bytes of memory, hard-disk drive, and printer cost less than $1,100 on the campus where we work. On-line access to indexes and abstract services has also proved to be far less expensive than originally thought. If the time of the reference librarian (or patron) is figured into the cost factors of on-line retrieval, often the use of on-line systems is lower than using the print resources, because so much more information can be searched so much faster.

The other factor that has made on-line access to indexes and abstract services viable for librarians has been the currency of the information found. Many on-line data bases now provide very current information. When the library patron wants the latest information, on-line access provides a way to provide that service. For libraries that attach a financial value to staff time expended (as in responding to a reference question or searching for a "correct" citation), on-line services easily justify their expense by saving staff time and effort.

Beyond the declining costs of technologies, librarians will want to consider the value of expanded services. Often technologically based information services provide access to information that would not be available in any other way. Most information (digital or visual) now being placed on large videodiscs is of a voluminous kind: all of the biology slides for education produced by major producers, the contents of major art museums, a video encyclopedia of the twentieth century.

Converting this information to videodisc format means that patron access to that information is increased. Patrons do not have to check volume after volume for a citation or illustration, do not have to manipulate volumes, do not have to go to the museum or original-source-document location.

In the same way, the many data bases, indexes, and full-text sources now available on-line allow all patrons and staff to browse in sources and deal with information they could not possibly have in their own libraries or homes. Where the search for information is done does not affect what information can be found. Many university faculty members and researchers now use on-line services, teleconferencing, and related services at their homes, while on trips, or at the office.

For disabled persons, many previously inaccessible resources will become available as libraries move into CD/ROM or videodisc formats and on-line formats. Once the materials are available for use with a microcomputer, the display can be enlarged for the visually impaired, colors may be modified for patrons with various forms of color blindness, and output can be changed from screen output to verbal output or Braille printout for later use. Large, inaccessible encyclopedias can be used by disabled children who could not see or hold the printed text. As full-text retrieval of periodicals and other serials becomes available on videodisc, access for the disabled will improve. Videodisc recording of pictures, slides, and various other visual displays previously inaccessible to disabled persons will become available on a large screen that can be operated by a hand-held digital control. These developments mean that information often thought to be inaccessible because of physical size or location can now be easily accessed from a keyboard or an adaptive device (such as a microcomputer "mouse").

SUMMARY

This chapter has discussed some of the newer technologies that will surely influence library programs and services. The impact of these developments for disabled persons was outlined. If librarians adopt new ways of providing information to their patrons, disabled persons may benefit from these technologies. The information-delivery systems of the future will certainly be more adaptable to a wide variety of patrons and library staff members.

REFERENCES

Avollone, S., and Fox, B. L. 1986. A commitment to cassettes. *Library Journal* 111(19), 35–37.

Carney, R. 1985. Information access company's InfoTrac. *Information Technology and Libraries* 4(2) 149–154.

Cash, J. 1985. Spinning toward the future: The museum on laser videodisc. *Museum News* 63(6).

Gale, J. C. 1985. The information workstation: A confluence of technologies including the CD-ROM. *Information Technology and Libraries* 4(2), 137–139.

Julien, D. 1985. Pioneering new services: Videocassettes. *Wilson Library Bulletin* 59(10), 664–667.

Kenney, B. L. 1983. *The status of cable communication in libraries.* Washington, DC: Council on Library Resources. ERIC Document Reproduction Service no. ED 095 841.

Lettner, L. L., et al. 1985. Videocassettes in libraries; library use of books on audiocassettes; and a videocassette circuit on a shoestring. *Library Journal* 110(19), 35–41.

Michaels, A. 1987. Design today. *Wilson Library Bulletin* 62(1), 56–59.

Miller, D. C. 1987. *Special report: Publishers, libraries & CD-ROM: Implications of digital optical publishing.* Chicago: American Library Association, Library and Information Technology Association.

Miller, R. B. 1983. Radiation, ergonomics, ion depletion, and VDTs: Healthful use of visual display terminals. *Information Technology and Libraries* 2(2), 151–158.

Ming, M. 1986. *A cooperative project for the development and delivery of training to rural library staff across Alberta. Phase two/three. Second interim report.* Edmonton: Southern Alberta Institute of Technology, Calgary. ERIC Document Reproduction Service, no. ED 272 210.

———, and MacDonald, G. 1987. Rural library training: Bridging the distance effectively. *Canadian Library Journal* 44(2), 73–78.

Murphy, B. 1985. CD/ROM and libraries. *Library Hi-tech* 3(2), 21–26.

Parker, E. B. 1985. The Library of Congress non-print optical disk pilot program. *Information technology and libraries* 4(4), 289–299.

Pifer, A., and Bronte, L., eds. 1986. *Our aging society: Paradox and promise.* New York: Norton.

Price-Wilkins, J. 1987. OPTEXT: Government publication on CD-ROM. *Reference Service Review* 15(2), 9–14.

Videodisc and optical disk technologies and their applications in libraries: A report to the Council on Library Resources. 1985. Washington, DC: Council on Library Resources.

Appendix A
Organizations and Agencies Serving
Disabled Children and Adults
and Their Families

National Organizations

Accent on Information
P.O. Box 700
Bloomington, IL 61701

Alexander Graham Bell Association for the Deaf
341 Volta Place NW
Washington, DC 20007-2778
(202-370-5220)

Allergy Foundation of America
118-35 Queens Blvd.
Forest Hills, NY 11375
(718-261-3633)

AMC Cancer Information Center
1600 Pierce St.
Lakewood, CO 80214
(800-525-3777)

American Association on Mental Deficiency
5101 Wisconsin Ave., NW
Washington, DC 20016

American Bar Association Child Advocacy Center
Suite 200, 1800 M. St., NW
Washington, DC 20036

American Cancer Society
4 W. 35th St.
New York, NY 10001
(212-736-3030)

American Coalition of Citizens with Disabilities
1200 15th St., NW
Washington, DC 20016

119

American Council for Rural Special Education
Western Washington University
Bellingham, WA 98225
(206-676-2576)

American Council of the Blind
Suite 1100
1010 Vermont Ave., NW
Washington, DC 20005
(800-424-8666)

American Diabetes Association
National Service Center
1660 Duke St.
Alexandria, VA 22314
(800-232-3472)

American Foundation for the Blind
15 W. 16th St.
New York, NY 10011
(212-620-2000)

American Heart Association
7320 Greenville Ave.
Dallas, TX 75231
(214-750-5300)

American Juvenile Arthritis Organization,
Arthritis Foundation National Office
1314 Spring St., NW
Atlanta, GA 30309
(404-872-7100)

American Kidney Fund
7315 Wisconsin Ave.
Bethesda, MD 20814-3266
(800-638-8299)

American Library Association
Association of Specialized and Cooperative Library Agencies
50 E. Huron St.
Chicago, IL 60611

American Lung Association
1740 Broadway
New York, NY 10019
(212-315-8700)

American Lupus Society
23751 Madison St.
Torrance, CA 90505
(213-373-1335)

American Printing House for the Blind
P.O. Box 6085
1839 Frankfurt Ave.
Louisville, KY 40206
(502-895-2405)

American Society for Deaf Children
814 Thayer Ave.
Silver Spring, MD 20910
(301-585-5400)

American Tuberous Sclerosis Association
39 Union St.
P.O. Box 44
Rockland, MA 02370
(800-446-1211)

Association for Children with Down's Syndrome
2616 Martin Ave.
Bellmore, NY 11710
(516-221-4700)

Association for Children with Learning Disabilities
4156 Library Rd.
Pittsburgh, PA 15234
(412-341-8077)

Association for Persons with Severe Handicaps
7010 Roosevelt Way, NE
Seattle, WA 98115
(206-523-8446)

Association for Retarded Citizens of the U.S.
2501 Ave. J
Arlington, TX 76011
(800-433-5255)

Association of Birth Defect Children
3526 Emerywood Lane
Orlando, FL 32806
(305-859-2821)

Asthma and Allergy Foundation of America
1302 18th St., NW
Washington, DC 20036
(202-293-2950)

Better Hearing Institute Hearing Helpline
1430 K St., NW
Suite 700
Washington, DC 20005
(800-424-8576)

Canadian Association for the Mentally Retarded
National Institute on Mental Retardation
8605 Rue Berri, Bureau 300
Montreal, Quebec
Canada H2P 2G5
(514-281-2307)

Canadian Cerebral Palsy Association
500 Bloor St. E.
Suite 301
Toronto, Ontario
Canada M4W 1A9
(416-923-2932)

Canadian Diabetes Association
78 Bond St.
Toronto, Ontario
Canada M5B 2J8
(416-362-4440)

Canadian Hearing Society
271 Spadina Rd.
Toronto, Ontario
Canada M5R 2V3
(416-964-2066)

Canadian Hemophilia Society
100 King St. W.
Hamilton, Ontario
Canada L8P 1A2
(416-523-6214)

Canadian National Institute for the Blind
1929 Bayview Ave.
Toronto, Ontario
Canada M4G 3E8

Canadian Rehabilitation Council for the Disabled
One Yonge St.
Suite 210
Toronto, Ontario
Canada M5E 1E5
(416-862-0340)

Cancer Information Clearinghouse
National Cancer Institute
9000 Rockefeller Pike
Building 31, RM10A21
Bethesda, MD 20205
(800-422-6237)

Candlelighters Childhood Cancer Society
2025 Eye St., NW
Suite 1011
Washington, DC 20006
(202-659-5136)

Caring Inc.
P.O. Box 400
Milton, WA 98354
(206-922-8194)

Children's Brain Diseases
Foundation for Research
350 Parnassus
Suite 900
San Francisco, CA
(415-566-6259)

Children's Defense Fund
122 C St., NW
Washington, DC 20001
(800-424-9602)

Children's Hearing Foundation
220 S. 16th St.
Philadelphia, PA 19102

Children's Hospice International
1800 Diagonal Rd. 600
Alexandria, VA 22314
(703-684-4464)

Children's Liver Foundation, Inc.
155 Maplewood Ave.
Maplewood, NJ 07040
(201-761-1111)

Closer Look/Parent's Campaign for Handicapped Children
1201 16th St. NW
Suite 233
Washington, DC 20036
(800-522-3458)

CMT International (Charcot-Marie-Tooth Disease)
34-B Bayview Dr.
St. Catherines, Ontario
Canada L2N 4Y6

Coalition on Sexuality and Disability, Inc.
853 Broadway
Suite 611
New York, NY 10003
(212-242-3900)

Compassionate Friends Inc.
Box 3696
Oak Park, IL 60522-3696
(312-323-5010)

Congress of Organization for the Physically Handicapped
16630 Beverly Ave.
Tinley Park, IL 60477-1904
(312-532-3566)

Cornelia De Lange Syndrome Foundation
60 Dyer Ave.
Collinsville, CT 06022
(800-223-8355)

Council for Exceptional Children
1920 Association Drive
Reston, VA 22091

Cystic Fibrosis Foundation
6000 Executive Blvd.
Suite 510
Rockville, MD 20852
(800-638-8815)

Digestive Diseases Clearinghouse
1255 23rd St. NW #275
Washington, DC 20037

Disability Rights Education and Defense Fund, Inc.
1616 P St., NW
Suite 100
Washington, DC 20036
(202-328-5185)

Dystonia Foundation, Inc.
370 Lexington Ave.
Room 1504
New York, NY 10017
(212-924-0682)

Dystonia Medical Research Foundation
First City Building, Suite 1800
777 Hornby St.
Vancouver, B.C.
Canada V6Z 1S4
(604-661-4886)

Epilepsy Foundation of America
4351 Garden City Drive
Landover, MD 20785
(301-459-3700)

Especially Grandparents
The Grandparents Program
ARC of King County
2230 Eighth Ave.
Seattle, WA 98121

Families of Spinal Muscular Atrophy
P.O. Box 1465
Highland Park, IL 60035
(312-432-5551)

Foundation for Children with Learning Disabilities
P.O. Box 2929
Grand Central Station
New York, NY 10163
(212-687-7211)

Friedreich's Ataxia Group in America, Inc.
P.O. Box 1116
Oakland, CA 94611
(415-655-0833)

Guardians of Hydrocephalus Research Foundation
2618 Ave. Z
Brooklyn, NY 11235
(718-743-4473)

Help for Incontinent People (HIP)
P.O. Box 544
Union, SC 29379

Human Resources Center
I. U. Willits Rd.
Albertson, NY 11507

Hydrocephalus Support Group
225 Dickinson St., H-893
San Diego, CA 92103
(619-695-3139)

Immune Deficiency Foundation
P.O. Box 586
Columbia, ND 21045
(301-461-3127)

International Parents Organization SEE
Alexander Graham Bell Association for the Deaf

International Rett Syndrome Association
8511 Rose Marie Drive
Fort Washington, MD 20744
(301-248-7031)

International Shriners Headquarters
P.O. Box 25356
Tampa, FL 33622
(800-237-5055)

Intraventricular Hemorrhage Parents
P.O. Box 56-111
Miami, FL 33156
(305-232-0381)

Juvenile Diabetes Foundation International
60 Madison Ave.
New York, NY 10010
(800-223-1138)

Kinsmen Rehabilitation Foundation of British Columbia
2256 W. 12 Ave.
Vancouver, B.C.
Canada V6K 2N5
(604-736-8411)

Laurence-Moon-Biedel Syndrome Network
122 Rolling Rd.
Lexington Park, MD 20653
(301-863-5658)

Leukemia Society of America
733 Third Ave.
14th Floor
New York, NY 10017
(212-573-8484)

Little People of America, Inc.
P.O. Box 633
San Bruno, CA 94066
(415-589-0695)

Lowe's Syndrome Association
222 Lincoln St.
West Lafayette, IN 47906
(317-743-3634)

Lupus Foundation of America, Inc.
11921-A Olive Blvd.
St. Louis, MO 63141
(314-872-9036)

Maple Syrup Urine Disease Support Group
24806 Sr 119
Goshen, IN 46526
(219-862-2922)
            or
RR 2 Box 24A
Flemingsburg, KY 41041
(606-849-4679)

March of Dimes Birth Defects Foundation
1275 Mamaroneck Ave.
White Plains, NY 10605
(914-428-7100)

Metabolic Illness Foundation
210 S. Furth St.
Monroe, LA 71202
(318-343-0416)

Muscular Dystrophy Association
810 Seventh Ave.
New York, NY 10019
(212-586-0808)

National Amputation Foundation
12-45 150th St.
Whitestone, NY 11357
(718-767-0596)

National Association for Hearing and Speech Action
Rockville, MD 20852
(800-638-8255)

National Association for Parents of the Visually Impaired
P.O. Box 180806
Austin, TX 78718
(512-459-6651)

National Association for Sickle Cell Disease
4221 Wilshire Blvd.
Suite 360
Los Angeles, CA 90010-3503
(800-421-8453)

National Association for Visually Handicapped
22 W. 21st St.
Sixth Floor
New York, NY 10010
(212-889-3141)

National Association of Mothers of Special Children
9079 Arrowhead Court
Cincinnati, OH 45231

National Association of the Deaf
814 Thayer Ave.
Silver Spring, MD 20910
(301-587-1788)

National Association of the Physically Handicapped
1601 N. College-71
Fort Collins, CO 80524

National Ataxia Foundation
600 Twelve Oaks Center
15500 Wayzata Blvd.
Wayzata, MN 55391
(612-473-7666)

National Autism Hotline
Autism Services Center
Douglass Education Building
Tenth Ave. & Bruce
Huntington, WV 25701
(304-525-8014)

National Birth Defects Center
20 Warren St.
Brighton, MA 02135
(617-787-5958)

National Captioning Institute
5203 Leesburg Pike
Falls Church, VA 22041
(800-528-6600)

National Center for Education in Maternal and Child Care
38th & R Sts. NW
Washington, DC 20057
(202-625-8400)

National Center for Stuttering
200 E. 33rd St.
New York, NY 10016
(800-221-2483)

National Center for the
Prevention of Sudden Infant Death Syndrome
330 N. Charles St.
Baltimore, MD 21201
(800-638-7437)

National Center for Youth with Disabilities
Adolescent Health Program
Box 721
University of Minnesota
Minneapolis, MN 55455
(612-626-2796)

National Cleft Palate Association
906 Hillside Lane
Flower Mound, TX 75028
(316-543-6623)

National Crisis Center for the Deaf
Box 484
UVA Medical Center
Charlottesville, VA 22908
(800-466-9876)

National Down's Syndrome Congress
1800 Dempster St.
Park Ridge, IL 60608-114
(800-232-6372)

National Down's Syndrome Society
141 Fifth Ave.
New York, NY 10010
(800-221-4602)

National Easter Seal Society
2023 W. Ogden Ave.
Chicago, IL 60612
(800-221-6827)

National Federation of the Blind
1800 Johnson St.
Baltimore, MD 21230
(301-659-9314)

National Foundation for Asthma, Inc.
P.O. Box 3006
Tucson AZ 85751-0069
(602-323-6046)

National Foundation for Ileitis and Colitis
444 Park Ave. S.
New York, NY 10016
(212-685-3400)

National Foundation for Peroneal Muscular Atrophy
University City Science Center
3624 Market St.
Philadelphia, PA 19104
(215-387-2255)

National Genetics Foundation, Inc.
555 W. 57th St.
New York, NY 10019
(212-586-5800)

National Head Injury Association
P.O. Box 567
Framingham, MA 01701
(617-879-7473)

National Health Information Clearinghouse
P.O. Box 1133
Washington, DC 20013-1133

National Hearing Aid Society
20361 Middlebelt
Livonia, MI 48152
(800-521-5247)

National Hemophilia Foundation
The Soho Building
110 Greene St.
Room 406
New York, NY 10002
(212-219-8180)

National Hemophilia Foundation
Route 1, River Rd.
Box 210 A
Joliet, IL 60436

National Icthyosis Foundation
P.O. Box 252
Belmont, CA 94002
(415-591-1653)

National Information Center for Handicapped
Children and Youth
Box 1492
Washington, DC 20013

National Information Center for
Orphan Drugs and Rare Diseases
P.O. Box 1133
Washington, DC 20013-1133

National Information Center on Deafness
Gallaudet University
800 Florida Ave., NE
Washington, DC 20002
(202-651-5109)

National Institute for Rehabilitation Engineering
97 Decker Rd.
Butler, NJ 07405
(201-838-2500)

National Kidney Foundation, Inc.
2 Park Ave.
New York, NY 10016
(212-892-2210)

National Library Service for the Blind
and Physically Handicapped
1291 Taylor St., NW
Washington, DC 20542

National Media Council on Disability
c/o National Challenge Committee of the Disabled
1101 15th St. NW
Washington, DC 20005

National Mucopolysaccharidoses Society
17 Kraemer St.
Hicksville, NY 11801
(516-931-6338)

National Multiple Sclerosis Society
205 E. 42nd St.
New York, NY 10017
(212-986-3240)

National Network to Prevent Birth Defects
P.O. Box 15309
Washington, DC 20003
(202-543-5450)

National Neurofibromatosis Foundation, Inc.
141 Fifth Ave.
Suite 7-S
New York, NY 10010
(212-460-8980)

National Organization for Albinism and Hypopigmentation
909 Walnut St.
Room 400
Philadelphia, PA 19107
(215-627-0600)

National Organization for Rare Disorders
P.O. Box 8923
New Fairfield, CT 06812
(203-746-6518)

National Organization on Disability
2100 Pennsylvania Ave., NW
Washington, DC 20037

National Parent CHAIN, Inc.
867C High St.
Worthington, OH 43085
(614-431-1911)

National Parkinson Foundation
1501 NW Ninth Ave.
Miami, FL 33136
(800-327-4545)

National Rehabilitation Association
633 S. Washington St.
Alexandria, VA 23313
(703-836-0850)

National Rehabilitation Information Center (NARIC)
4407 Eighth St., NE
Washington, DC 20017

National Reye's Syndrome Foundation
426 N. Lewis
Bryan, OH 43506
(419-636-2679)

National Scoliosis Foundation
P.O. Box 547
93 Concord Ave.
Belmont, MA 02178
(617-489-0888)

National Sickle Cell Clinics Foundation, Inc.
P.O. Box 8095
Houston, TX 77288
(713-527-8236)

Appendix A

National Society for Children and Adults with Autism
1234 Massachusetts Ave., NW
Washington, DC 20005
(202-783-0125)

National Society to Prevent Blindness
79 Madison Ave.
New York, NY 10016
(212-684-3505)

National Spinal Cord Injury Association
149 California St.
Newton, MA 02158
(800-962-9629)

National Spinal Cord Injury Hotline
22 S. Greene St.
Baltimore, MD 21201
(800-526-3456)

National Stuttering Project
1269 Seventh Ave.
San Francisco, CA 94122
(425-566-5324)

National Sudden Infant Death Syndrome Foundation, Inc.
8240 Professional Place
Suite 205
Landover, MD 20785
(301-459-3388)

National Tay-Sachs and Allied Diseases Association
385 Elliot St.
Newton, MA 02164
(617-964-5508)

National Technical Institute for the Deaf
One Lomb Memorial Drive
Rochester, NY 14623

National Tuberous Sclerosis Association, Inc.
P.O. Box 612
Winfield, IL 60190
(312-668-0787)

Organization for Parents of Cleft Children
10 Carlsbad St.
Kenner, LA 70065

Orton Dyslexia Society
724 York Road
Baltimore, MD 21204
(800-222-3123)

Osteogenesis Imperfecta Foundation, Inc.
P.O. Box 245
Eastport, NY 11941

Paralyzed Veterans of America
801 18th St. NW
Washington, DC 20006
(202-259-1654)

Parents of Cataract Kids
179 Hunter's Lane
Devon, PA 19333
(215-293-1917)

Parents of Dwarfed Children
11524 Colt Terrace
Silver Spring, MD 20902
(301-649-3275)

Parents of John Tracy Clinic
806 W. Adams Blvd.
Los Angeles, CA 90007
(213-748-5481)

Parents of Twins with Disabilities
2129 Clinton Ave., #E
Alameda, CA 94501

People-to-People Committee on the Employment
of the Handicapped
1111 20th St., NW
Washington, DC 20210

Prader-Willi Syndrome Association
5515 Malibu Drive
Edina, MN 55436
(612-933-0113)

Prescription Parents, Inc. (Cleft Palate)
P.O. Box 426
Quincy, MA 02269
(617-479-2463)

Recording for the Blind, Inc.
20 Roszel Rd.
Princeton, NJ 08540

Regional Resource and Information Center
for Disabled Individuals
Moss Rehabilitation Hospital
12th St. and Tabor Rd.
Philadelphia, PA 19141

Rehabilitation International
25 E. 21st St.
New York, NY 10010
(212-420-1500)

Retinitis Pigmentosa Association International
23241 Ventura Blvd.
Woodland Hills, CA 91364
(800-344-4877)

Retinitis Pigmentosa Foundation Fighting Blindness
1401 Mt. Royal Ave.
Fourth Floor
Baltimore, MD 21217
(800-638-2300)

Self-Help for Hard of Hearing People
7800 Wisconsin Ave.
Bethesda, MD 20814
(301-657-2248)

Sick Kids Need Involved People (SKIP)
216 Newport Drive
Severna Park, MD 21146
(301-647-0164)

Society for the Rehabilitation of the
Facially Disfigured
550 First Ave.
New York, NY 10016
(212-340-6656)

Spina Bifida Association of America
343 S. Dearborn, Suite 317
Chicago, IL 60604
(800-621-3141)

Spina Bifida Association of Canada
633 Willington Crescent
Winnipeg, Manitoba
Canada R3M OA8
(204-521-7580)

Support Group for Trisomy 18/13
c/o Kris & Hal Holladay
478 Terrace Lane
Tooele, UT 84074
(801-882-6635)

Tourette Syndrome Association
2001 Ford Center #6
Milford, OH 45150-2713

Tripod — Service for Hearing Impaired
955 N. Alfred St.
Los Angeles, CA 90069
(213-656-4904)

Turner's Syndrome Society
Administrative Studies #006
4700 Keele St.
York University
Downsview, Ontario
Canada M3J 1P3
(426-667-3773)

United Cerebral Palsy Association
2304 Highland Drive
New York, NY 10016
(212-481-6300)

United Lekodystrophy
44105 Yorkshire Drive
Wayne, MI 48184-2859

United Lekodystrophy Foundation, Inc.
2304 Highland Drive
Sycamore, IL 60178
(815-895-3211)

United Ostomy Association, Inc.
2001 W. Beverly Blvd.
Los Angeles, CA 90057
(213-413-5510)

Williams Syndrome Association
P.O. Box 17873
San Diego, CA 92117-0910
(691-275-6628)

Organizations in Recreation

4–H Youth Development Extension Service
Room 3860–S
U.S. Department of Agriculture
Washington, DC 20250
(202-447-5853)

American Alliance for Health, Physical Education,
Recreation and Dance
1900 Association Drive
Reston, VA 22091
(703-476-3400)

American Athletic Association of the Deaf
3916 Lantern Drive
Silver Spring, MD 20902

American Blind Bowling Association
c/o Gilbert Baqui
3500 Terry Drive
Norfolk, VA 23518
(804-857-7267)

American Camping Association
5000 State Road
Martinsville, IN 46151
(317-342-8456)

American Wheelchair Bowling Association
N54 W15858 Larkspur Lane
Menomonee Falls, WI 53501

Boy Scouts of America
Scouting for the Handicapped
1325 Walnut Hill Lane
Irving, TX 75038-3096
(214-659-2127)

California Wheelchair Aviators
117 Rising Hill
Escondido, CA 92025

Canadian Recreational Canoeing Association
P.O. Box 500
Hyde Park, Ontario
Canada NOM 1ZZ0
(591-473-2109)

Canadian Wheelchair Sports Association
333 River Road
Ottawa, Ontario
Canada K1L 8B9
(613-748-6128)

Committee for the Promotion of Camping
for the Handicapped
830 Third Ave.
New York, NY 10022
(212-940-7500)

Disabled Sportsmen of America
P.O. Box 5496
Roanoke, VA 24012

Handicapped Scuba Association
1104 El Prado
San Clemente, CA 92672
(714-498-6128)

International Committee of the Silent Sports
800 Florida Ave., NE
Washington, DC 20002
(202-651-5114)

International Foundations for Wheelchair Tennis
2203 Timberloch Place
Suite 126
The Woodlands, TX 77380
(713-363-4707)

International Wheelchair Road Racers Club
16578 Ave. NE
St. Petersburg, FL 33702

Let's Play to Grow
1350 New York Ave.
Suite 500
Washington, DC 20005-4709
(202-393-1250)

National Archery Association
1750 E. Boulder St.
Colorado Springs, CO 80909
(303-578-4576)

National Association for Sports for Cerebral Palsy
66 E. 34th St.
New York, NY 10016
(212-481-6359)

National Foundation of Wheelchair Tennis
15441 Redhill Ave.
Suite A
Tustin, CA 92680
(714-259-1531)

National Handicap Sports and Recreation Association
P.O. Box 33141, Farragut Station
Washington, DC 20033
(202-429-0595)

National Handicapped Sports and Recreation Association
Capital Hill Station
P.O. Box 18664
Denver, CO 80218
(303-632-0698)

National Junior Horticultural Association
c/o American Horticultural Society
P.O. Box 0105
Mount Vernon, VA 22121
(703-768-5700)

National Park Service
Division of Special Programs and Populations
Department of Interior
18th & C St., NW
Washington, DC 20240
(202-343-4747)

National Therapeutic Recreation Society
3101 Park Center Drive
Alexandria, VA 22302
(703-820-4940)

National Wheelchair Athletic Association
3617 Betty Drive
Suite S
Colorado Springs, CO 80907
(303-632-0698)

National Wheelchair Basketball Association
c/o AARAA
815 Weber
Suite 203
Colorado Springs, CO 80903

National Wheelchair Racketball Association
P.O. Box 737
Sioux Falls, SD 57101

North American Riding for the Handicapped
111 E. Wacker Drive
Chicago, IL 60601
(312-644-6610)

Paralyzed Veterans of America
801 18th St. NW
Washington, DC 20006
(202-872-1300)

Ski for Light
c/o Bud Keith
737 North Buchanan St.
Arlington, VA 22203

Special Olympics
Kennedy Foundation
1350 New York Ave.
Washington, DC 20005

United States Amputee Association
Route 2, Country Lane
Fairview, TN 37062
(615-670-5453)

U.S.A. Toy Library Association
104 Wilmot
Suite 201
Deerfield, IL 60015
(312-940-8800)

United States Quad Rugby Association
311 Northwestern Drive
Grand Forks, ND 58301
(701-771-1961)

Vinland National Center
P.O. Box 308
Loretto, MN 55357
(612-479-3555)

Wheelchair Motorcycle Association
101 Torry St.
Brockton, MA 02401
(617-583-8614)

World Recreation Association of the Deaf
P.O. Box 7894
Van Nuys, CA 91409

Appendix B
Computer Hardware and Software for Disabled Persons: Sources of Technical and Practical Information

C-TEC, Computer Training and Evaluation Center
399 Sherman Ave., Suite 12
Palo Alto, CA 94304
(415-493-5000, Ext. 4375)
   Evaluates computer equipment for visually impaired people and provides training on that equipment.

Center for Special Education Technology/Exchange
Council for Exceptional Children
1920 Association Drive
Reston, VA 22091
(800-345-8324)
   Promotes the systematic collection and transfer of information about technology advances and applications among parents, educators, and administrators. Issues reports and publishes information through the CEC network.

Center for Technology in Human Disabilities
c/o Division of Education
Johns Hopkins University
Baltimore, MD 21205
(301-338-8273)
   Disseminates information about technological applications for the disabled as well as diagnostic and consultative services to individuals to promote independent living. Research-and-development projects related to rehabilitation.

CTG Solutions c/o Closing the Gap
P.O. Box 68
Henderson, MN 56044
(612-248-3294)
   Provides information on how to use products and applications of computer technology relevant to special education and rehabilitation as identified by *Closing the Gap* over the past five years. Includes names of products, prices, special skills required, skill level, peripherals, adaptive devices.

Disabled Children's Computer Group
Fairmont School
724 Kearney St.
El Cerrito, CA 94530
(415-528-3224)
> Operates an equipment resource center and a computer bulletin board about equipment and the availability of money to buy it.

Institute for Technology in the Education
and Rehabilitation of the Visually Impaired
Department of Special Education
Teachers College
Columbia University
515 W. 120th St.
New York, NY 10027
(212-678-3873)
> Offers information about available equipment and holds a week-long symposium that includes demonstrations of equipment for the visually impaired (each summer).

National Braille Press, Inc.
National Technology Center
American Foundation for the Blind
15 West 16th St.
New York, NY 10011
(212-620-2020)
> Provides visually impaired students with access to educational materials that interact with computer technology; evaluates new and existing devices; provides information on consumer products, training courses, funding sources, and names and comments of current users of adaptive equipment. Publishes *Products for People with Vision Problems* annually.

Special Education Software Center
(800-327-5892)
> Provdes free information about computer software designed for use with special education students.

Special Net
National Association of State Directors of Special Education
2021 K St., NW
Suite 315
Washington, DC 20006
(202-296-1800)
> Offers a computer-based communication network designed to provide up-to-date information about special education programs and educational programs for students with disabilities.

Technical Resources Centre
1820 Richmond Rd., SW
Calgary, Alberta
Canada T2T 5C7
(403-229-7875)
> Provides information on devices in the areas of adaptive toys, communication aids for daily living, and microcomputers.

The Trace Center
Waisman Center
1500 Highland Ave.
Madison, WI 53705
(608-262-6966)
> Designs computer adaptations for children and adults. Research and evaluation of various adaptive aids for computing. Publishes *Information on Communication, Control, and Computer Access for Handicapped Individuals.*

Information Clearinghouses

ABLEDATA/REHAB DATA
National Rehabilitation Information Center (NARIC)
The Catholic University of America
4407 Eighth St., NE
Washington, DC 20017-2299
(202-635-5884)

Accent on Information
(309-378-2961)

Association for Special Education Technology
P.O. Box 152
Allen, TX 75002
(214-339-2858)

Center for Special Education Technology
Council for Exceptional Children
1920 Association Drive
Reston, VA 22091
(800-345-8324)

Committee on Personal Computers and the Handicapped (COPH-2)
2030 Irving Park Road
Chicago, IL 60618
(312-477-1813)

CompuHelp
National Association of Blind and Visually
Impaired Computer Users
(916-786-3923)

Computers Users in Speech and Hearing
Department of Speech Pathology and Audiology
University of South Alabama
Mobile, AL 36688
(205-460-3727)

DEAFNET
SRI International
333 Ravenwood Ave.
Menlo Park, CA 94025
(415-326-6200)

Handicapped Users' Database
CompuServe, Inc.
(800-848-8199)

National Support Center for
Persons with Disabilities
IBM Educational Systems
4111 Northside Parkway
Atlanta, GA 30327
(800-IBM-2133)

Office of Special Education Program
Apple Computer, Inc.
20527 Mariani Ave.
Cupertino, CA 95014
(408-973-6484)

Rural Rehabilitation Technologies Database
University of North Dakota
(701-780-2489)

Special Education Software Center
LINC Resources, Inc.
3857 N. High St.
Columbus, OH 43214
(800-327-5892)

SpecialNet
National Association of State
Directors of Special Education
2021 K St., NW
Suite 315
Washington, DC 20006

Technical Resource Center
1820 Richmond Road, SW
Calgary, Alberta
Canada T2T 5C7

Publications

Add-Ons
National Braille Press, Inc.
American Foundation for the Blind
15 West 16th St.
New York, NY 10011
(212-620-2020)

Augmentative and Alternative Communication Journal
428 E. Preston St.
Baltimore, MD 21202

Bulletin of Science and Technology for the Handicapped
1776 Massachusetts Ave., NW
Washington, DC 20036

Byte
70 Main St.
Peterborough, NH 03458

Closing the Gap
P.O. Box 68
Henderson, MN 56044

Communication Outlook
Artificial Language Laboratory
Michigan State University
East Lansing, MI 48824

Computer Disability News
National Easter Seal Society
2023 W. Ogden Ave.
Chicago, IL 60612

Computing Teacher
International Council for Computers in Education
University of Oregon
Eugene, OR 97403-1923

COPH Bulletin
2030 Irving Park Road
Chicago, IL 60618

Education Computer News
1300 N. 17th St.
Arlington, VA 22209

Journal of Special Education Technology
UMC 68, Utah State University
Logan, UT 84322

Software Directory for Communication Sciences and Disorders
American Speech-Language-Hearing Association
(301-897-5700)

The Special Directory
LINC Resources, Inc.
(614-263-5462)

Special Education Software Review
Dea Pfeiffer, Editor
(309-685-8262)

Special Times
Cambridge Development Laboratory
(800-637-0047)

Specialware Directory: A Guide to Software for Special Education
The Oryx Press
(602-254-6156)

Survey of Existing Software
Education Turnkey Systems, Inc.
(703-536-2310)

Appendix C
Commercial Vendors of Computers
and Related Materials for the Disabled

Adaptive Aids, Inc.
P.O. Box 57640
Tucson, AZ 85713
(800-233-5369 Ext. 357)
 Adaptive aids for physically disabled.

Adaptive Communication Systems
P.O. Box 12440
Pittsburgh, PA 15231
(412-264-2288)
 Software, adaptive aids, communication aids.

Adaptive Peripherals
4529 Bagley Ave., N
Seattle, WA 98103
(206-633-2610)
 Hardware, software, adaptive aids for physically disabled.

Aesir Software Engineering
P.O. Box 3583
Pinedale, CA 93650-3583
 Software, communication aids.

American Communication Corp.
180 Roberts St.
East Hartford, CT 06108
(203-289-3491)
 Adaptive aids for the hearing impaired.

American Thermoform Corp.
2311 Travers Ave.
City of Commerce, CA 90040
(213-723-9021)
 Adaptive aids for the visually impaired.

Apple Computer, Inc.
20515 Mariani Ave.
Cupertino, CA 95014
(408-996-1010)

Aquarious People Materials, Inc.
P.O. Box 128
Indian Rocks Beach, FL 33535
(813-595-7890)
Software for the mentally retarded.

Artic Technologies
2234 Star Court
Auburn Heights, MI 48057
(313-852-8344)
Adaptive aids for the visually impaired.

Artificial Language Laboratory Department of Audiology and Speech
Michigan State University
405 Computer Center
East Lansing, MI 48824
(517-353-5399)
Hardware, software, communication aids for the speech impaired.

Arts Computer Products, Inc.
145 Tremont St.   Suite 407
Boston, MA 02111
(617-482-8248)
Software for the visually impaired.

Audiobionics
9817 Valley View Rd.
Eaden Praire, MN 55344
(800-328-4827 Ext. 1400)
Software for the speech impaired.

Cacti Computer Services
130 Ninth St., SW
Portage La Praire, Manitoba
Canada R1N 2N4
(204-857-8675)
Software, hardware, adaptive aids for various disabilities.

Canon U.S.A., Inc.
One Canon Plaza
Lake Success, NY 11042-9979
(516-488-6700)
Adaptive aids for the speech impaired.

Commodore Computer
1200 Wilson Drive
West Chester, PA 19380
(215-431-9100)

Communication Studies
Department of Speech
University of New Mexico
Box 3W
Las Cruces, NM 88003
(505-646-2801)
Communication aids for the speech impaired.

ComputAbility Corp.
101 Rt. 46E
Pine Brook, NJ 07058
(201-882-0171)
    Hardware, software, adaptive aids.

Compu-Tations, Inc.
P.O. Box 502
Troy, MI 48099
(313-689-5059)
    Software for education.

Computer Aids Corp.
124 W. Washington Blvd.
Lower Arcade
Fort Wayne, IN 46802
(219-422-2424)
    Adaptive aids for the visually impaired.

Computer Aids Marketing Dept.
O'Neil Enterprises
P.O. Box 3683
Springfield, MO 65808
(800-647-8255)

Computer Conversations
2350 N. Fourth St.
Columbus, OH 43202
(614-263-4324)
    Adaptive aids for the visually impaired.

Computers to Help People, Inc.
1221 W. Johnson St.
Madison, WI 53715
(608-257-5917)
    Software for the physically disabled.

Com-Tek
3457 W. 2700 South
Salt Lake City, UT 84115
(801-466-3463)
    Adaptive aids for the hearing impaired.

Covox, Inc.
675-D Conger St.
Eugene, OR 97402
(503-342-1271)
    Software, adaptive aids for the speech impaired.

Crestwood Co.
P.O. Box 4606
Milwaukee, WI 53204
(414-351-0311)
    Adaptive and communication aids.

Cross Educational Software
P.O. Box 034606
Rustin, LA 71270
(318-255-8921)

Cyberon Corp.
1175 Wendy Road
Ann Arbor, MI 48103
(313-665-8512)

DADA: Designing Aids for Disabled Adults
1024 Dupont St.
Toronto, Ontario
Canada M6H 2A2
   Adaptive aids.

Don Johnston Developmental Equipment
900 Winnetka Terrace
Lake Zurich, IL 60047
(312-438-3476)
   Software, adaptive aids, communication aids.

Educational Activities, Inc.
P.O. Box 392
Freeport, NY 11520
(516-223-4666)
   Software for education.

Educational Audiology Program
1077 S. Gilpin St.
Denver, CO 80209
(303-777-0740)
   Software for the hearing impaired.

Educational Media Corp.
P.O. Box 21311
Minneapolis, MN 55421
(612-636-5098)
   Software for education.

Educational Teaching Aids
199 Carpenter Ave.
Wheeling, IL 60090
(312-520-2500)
   Software, adaptive aids.

EKEG Electronic Co., Ltd.
P.O. Box 46199
Station G
Vancouver, BC
Canada V6R 4G5
(604-685-7817)
   Hardware for the physically disabled.

Expert Systems Software, Inc.
923 Van Leer Drive
Nashville, TN 37220
(615-298-4397)

Extensions for Independence
635-5 N. Twin Oaks Valley Rd.
San Marcos, CA 92069
(619-744-4083)
    Adaptive and communication aids.

Foley's Low Vision Aids
1357 E. David Road
Kettering, OH 45429
(513-294-2433)
    Hardware, adaptive aids for the visually impaired.

Furalletech Systems Corp.
Flexcom Division
P.O. Box 190
310 W. Zeller St.
North Liberty, IA 52317
(800-272-2227)
    Adaptive and communication aids for the speech impaired.

Genesis Computer Corp.
P.O. Box 152
Hellertown, PA 18055
(215-861-0850)
    Hardware, adaptive aids, communication aids.

Handicapped Children's Technological Services
P.O. Box 7
Foster, RI 02825
(401-861-3444)
    Hardware, software, adaptive aids.

Hartley Courseware, Inc.
P.O. Box 431
Dimondale, MI 48821
(800-247-1380)
    Software for education of the mentally retarded.

IBM
Old Orchard Road
Armonk, NY 10504
(914-765-1900)

Innocomp
22195 Wagon Wheel
Solon, OH 44139
(216-248-6206)
    Hardware, software, communication aids for the speech impaired.

Innovative Rehabilitation Technology, Inc.
26699 Snell Lane
Los Altos Hills, CA 94022
(415-948-8588)
    Adaptive aids, communication aids for the physically disabled.

Interstate Voice Products
1849 W. Sequoia Ave.
Orange, CA 92688
(714-937-9010)
    Communication aids.

Intex Micro Systems Corp.
725 S. Adams Road
Suite L8
Birmingham, MI 48011
(313-540-7601)

J. A. Preston Corp.
60 Page Rd.
Clifton, NJ 07012
(201-777-2700)
    Software, adaptive aids.

Jupiter Technology, Inc.
78 Fourth Ave.
Waltham, MA 02154
(617-890-4555)

K Talker Sales
P.O. Box 81082
Seattle, WA 98108
(206-722-8599)

Kay Elemetrics Corp.
12 Maple Ave.
Pine Brook, NJ 07058-9797
(201-227-2000)
    Software, hardware, communication aids.

Kurzweil Computer Products, Inc.
185 Albany St.
Cambridge, MA 02139
(800-343-0311)
    Adaptive and communication aids for the visually impaired.

Laureate Learning Systems, Inc.
Dept. A-17
One Mill St.
110 E Spring St.
Winooski, VT 05404-1828
    Software for the physically disabled and speech impaired.

Life Science Associates
1 Fenimore Road
Bayport, NY 11705
(516-472-2111)
  Software, adaptive aids.

Lou Price
10148 Lasso Lane
Shreveport, LA 71106
(318-226-7806)

McGraw-Hill
Gregg Division
1221 Avenue of the Americas
New York, NY 10020
(212-512-2000)
  Software for the physically disabled.

Maryland Computer Services
3132 SE Jay St.
Stuart, FL 33497
(305-288-2080)
  Hardware for the visually impaired.

MCE, Inc.
157 S. Kalamazoo Mall
Kalamazoo, MI 49007
(800-421-4157)
  Software for education.

MECC
3490 N. Lexington Ave.
St. Paul, MN 55126
(612-481-3500)
  Software for various disability groups.

Media Materials, Inc.
2936 Remington Ave.
Baltimore, MD 21211
(301-235-1700)
  Software for various disability groups.

Micro Video
210 Collingwood
Suite 100
Ann Arbor, MI 48107
(313-996-0626)
  Communication aids for the hearing impaired and visually impaired.

Micromint, Inc.
25 Terrace Drive
Vernon, CT 06066
(203-871-6170)
  Hardware for the physically disabled.

Microphonics
25 37th St. NE
Suite B
Auburn, WA 98002
(206-939-2321)
  Adaptive aids for the physically disabled.

Microtech Consulting Co.
P.O. Box 521
206 Angie Drive
Cedar Falls, IA 50613
(319-277-6648)

Optelec USA, Inc.
325 Ayer Road
Harvard, MA 01451
(617-772-9269)
  Adaptive aids for the visually impaired.

Palmetto Technologies
P.O. Box 498
Duncan, SC 29334
(803-576-2886)
  Adaptive and communication aids for the hearing impaired.

Peal Software
2210 Wilshire Blvd.
Suite 806
Santa Monica, CA 90403
(213-451-0997)
  Software for education.

Perkins School for the Blind
175 N. Beacon St.
Watertown, MA 02172
  Adaptive aids for the visually impaired.

Personal Microcomputers, Inc.
275 Santa Ana Court
Sunnyvale, CA 94086
(408-737-8444)
  Adaptive aids for the visually impaired.

Phone-TTY, Inc.
202 Lexington Ave.
Hackensack, NJ 07601
(201-489-7889)
  Hardware, communication aids for the hearing impaired.

Phonic Ear
250 Camino Alto
Mill Valley, CA 94941
  Communication aids.

Polytel
1250 Oakmead Parkway
Suite 310
Sunnyvale, CA 94086
(408-730-1347)
   Adaptive aids for the physically disabled.

Prentke Romich Co.
1022 Heyl Road
Wooster, OH 44691
(216-262-1984)
   Adaptive and communication aids for the physically disabled.

Prometheus Systems
551 Chesman St.
West Hempstead, NY 11552
(516-485-5491)
   Software for the physically disabled.

Psycho-Linguistic Research Associates
2055 Sterling Ave.
Menlo Park, CA 94025
(415-854-1771)

Psychological Software Service
P.O. Box 29205
Indianapolis, IN 46229
(317-257-9672)

R. J. Cooper and Associates
2144 SE 1100
Suite 150
Salt Lake City, UT 84106
(801-263-1388)

R/M Systems
22903 Fern Ave.
Torrance, CA 90505
(213-534-1880)
   Hardware, adaptive aids, communication aids.

Raised Dot Computing, Inc.
408 S. Baldwin St.
Madison, WI 53703
(608-257-9595)
   Software for Braille output.

Robert E. Stepp III
Station A
P.O. Box 5002
Champaign, IL 61820
(217-359-7933)

Scott Instruments
1111 Willow Springs Dr.
Denton, TX 76205
(817-387-9514)
   Hardware, software for education of the mentally retarded.

Sensory Aids Corp.
205 W. Grand Ave.
Suite 110
Bensonville, IL 60106
(312-766-3935)
   Software for the visually impaired.

Sentient Systems Technology, Inc.
5001 Baum Blvd.
Pittsburgh, PA 15213
(412-682-0144)
   Communication aids for the speech impaired.

Shea Products, Inc.
1042 W. Hamlin Rd.
Rochester, MI 48063
(313-656-2281)
   Communication aids for the speech impaired.

Sliwa Enterprises
111 Fielding Lewis Drive
P.O. Box 978
Grafton, VA 23692
(804-898-8386)
   Software for education.

Software Research Corp.
3939 Quadra St.
Victoria, B.C.
Canada V8X 1J5
   Software, communication aids for the speech impaired and the hearing impaired.

Special Soft Co.
P.O. Box 1983
Santa Monica, CA 90406
(213-215-1890)

Speech Plus, Inc.
P.O. Box 7461
Mountain View, CA 94039-7461
(415-964-7023)
   Software for the visually impaired.

Street Electronics Corp.
1140 Mark Ave.
Carpinteria, CA 93013
(805-684-4593)
   Hardware, communication aids for the visually impaired and the speech impaired.

Talking Computers, Inc.
6931 N. 27th Road
Arlington, VA 22213
(703-241-8224)
  Hardware for the visually impaired.

TASH, Inc.
70 Gibson Dr.
Unit 1
Markham, Ontario
Canada L3R 2Z3
(416-475-2212)
  Hardware, adaptive aids for the physically disabled and speech impaired.

Teacher Support Software
P.O. Box 7130
Gainesville, FL 32605
(904-371-3802)
  Software for education of the mentally retarded.

Teaching Pathways, Inc.
212 E. Second Ave.
Amarillo, TX 79101
(806-373-1847)
  Software for the mentally retarded.

Telecommunications for the Deaf
814 Thayer Ave.
Silver Spring, MD 20910
(301-589-3006)

Tele-Consumer Hotline
1536 16th St., NW
Washington, DC 20036
(800-332-1124)

Telesensory Systems, Inc.
455 N. Bernado Ave.
P.O. Box 7455
Mountainview, CA 94043-5724
(412-960-0920)
  Adaptive aids for the hearing impaired.

Telex Communications, Inc.
9600 Aldrich Ave., S.
Minneapolis, MN 55420
(612-884-4051)
  Adaptive aids for the hearing impaired.

Tiger Communication System, Inc.
155 E. Broad St., #325
Rochester, NY 14604
(716-454-5134)
  Hardware, software, communication aids.

Triformation Systems, Inc.
3102 SE Jan St.
Stuart, FL 33497
(305-283-4817)
Hardware for the visually impaired.

Typewriting Institute for the Handicapped
3102 W. Augusta Ave.
Phoenix, AZ 85021

Ultratec, Inc.
6442 Normandy Lane
Madison, WI 53719
(608-273-0707)
Adaptive aids for the hearing impaired.

Unicorn Engineering Co.
6201 Harwood Ave.
Oakland, CA 94618
(415-428-1626)
Hardware, adaptive aids, communication aids.

Universe Electric Research Co.
510 Florence
St. Louis, MO 63119
(314-961-7253)
Software for the hearing impaired.

Upper Room
1421 N. Broadway
Suite 109
Menomonie, WI 54751
(715-235-5775)
Software for the mentally retarded.

Voice Connection
17835 Skypark Circle
Suite C
Irvine, CA 92714
(415-490-7600)
Software, communication aids for the mentally retarded.

Votan
4487 Technology Drive
Freemont, CA 94538
(415-490-7600)
Hardware, software, communication aids.

Votrax, Inc.
1394 Rankin
Troy, MI 48083
(800-588-0341)
Communication aids.

Vtek, Inc.
1625 Olympic Blvd.
Santa Monica, CA 90404
(213-452-5966)
   Hardware, software for the mentally retarded.

Washington Research Foundation
1107 NE 45th St.
Suite 322
Seattle, WA 98105
(206-633-3569)
   Software for the mentally retarded.

West Midlands MEP Project
Four Dwellings School
Quinton
Birmingham, B3C 1R2
England

Words +
1125 Steward Ct.
Suite D
Sunnyvale, CA 94086
(408-730-9588)
   Communication aids.

Zygo Industries, Inc.
P.O. Box 1008
Portland, OR 92707
(503-297-1724)

Index